IntelligentRisking™
for Women

By Barbara Stoker

author of *A Woman with A Minute*

Thank You

A special acknowledgment to Valari Burger:
Valari has read and reread this book almost as many times as I have. She is, without a doubt, the only reason this book ever made it to print. Not only is she a fabulous friend, she is the best "task master" ever. Thank you, Valari, from the bottom of my heart.

A special acknowledgment to Brian O'Malley:
Brian is a former police officer, S.W.A.T. team member, and paramedic firefighter, as well as an Everest climber, award-winning photographer, author, and world-renowned lecturer. That's quite a background to bring to a conversation regarding risk. Many of the concepts in this book were born out of the lively, heated debates we have had over the years regarding how men and women look at risk differently. I must admit it's hard to argue too fiercely with the guy who's holding the rope while you climb. Brian, thank you for your patience, your support, and your belief in me.

A special acknowledgment to the fabulous women I have had the privilege to work with at Jackson Walker and Equity Office Properties: Thank you for your help, support and direction.

Dedication

I would never have been able to finish this book
were it not for those who have believed in me,
even when others-including myself-doubted:

Connor, my philosopher

Nick, my negotiator

Joey, my professor

Valari, my twin spirit

Brian, my friend

Suzy, my boss

Leslie, my mentor

ISBN #0-9746722-0-3

Illustrations by Lauren Raio and George O'Malley
Text design by Loneta Showell
Editing by Valari Burger and Michelle Asakawa
Published by IntelligentRisking,™ Inc.
Printed in Canada

www.IntelligentRisking.com

Everest by George O'Malley

Each of us faces challenges and goals with associated risks.
They are the mountains we must climb.

IntelligentRisking
turns the impossible into
the probable, becoming
the inevitable.

IntelligentRisking™
for Women

4 Simple Strategies

Taking the right risks in the smartest way possible

By Barbara Stoker

author of *A Woman with A Minute*

Contents

The Crux Move

"Security is mostly a superstition. It does not exist in nature,
nor do the children of men as a whole experience it.
Avoiding danger is no safer in the long run than outright exposure."
—Helen Keller

1. The Monster Within

My fingers are jammed into a tiny crack as I press the edge of my climbing shoe against a sliver of rock. This route is at the upper end of my skill range; a successful climb here will take me to the next level in my ability. I have been climbing strong today, but now I'm approaching the most important and difficult part of the climb. Navigate this overhang and I will make it to the top. Misjudge it, and the best I can hope for is to escape unscathed and call it a day. I'm at the pivotal point of any climb...known as the crux move.

I feel my right foot slipping. I shift my weight to rebalance. What was I thinking, picking a route this difficult? It's pointless to ask the mountain to be easier — I must become a better climber. Still, this space between comfort and challenge is hard.

I stop, take some deep breaths, and assess my situation. I'm two hundred feet above the ground with the full weight of my body supported by a quarter-inch of granite. The muscles in my calves are starting to quiver. Elvis is alive and his moves are in my legs. I'm under an overhang that juts seemingly into eternity. My heart races when I realize the tremendous amount of faith I've placed in my own abilities.

Time stands still as I try to cut a deal with this rock. Adrenaline races through my body; my lips and mouth are dry. Strategy is as critical as execution. Quickly I determine the next few moves that will get me through the crux. This is a chess game played on a granite board with a stopwatch ticking. I move into position under the roof.

I waver for an instant, and for the first time I wonder if I'm in over my head. In that moment of self-doubt, I hear a haunting whisper from the monster that hides in the recesses of my mind:

"This is beyond you. You're not good enough-if you move, you'll fall." Now that I've allowed myself to hear the monster within taunting me, I can't stop listening. The voice grows louder. "You don't have what it takes. You'd better quit." I tell myself that this voice of the monster within is only my own self-induced sabotage.

I know from past experience that even though these next few moves are risky, taking the time to indulge my doubts poses an even greater risk, an Invisible Risk. I need all the energy I have, and the clock is running. Every second I waste listening to that voice, I burn up precious strength. Hesitating and "holding on" virtually sentences me to a fall. My arms are screaming. I am balanced on a pencil-width of rock. Now I realize I can't see above the rock to find a handhold. How much more difficult can this get? I must make a "blind move" or the climb ends here. Somehow, I've got to find the guts to leave this very slim margin of safety.

If I move, I may fall, but if I don't move, I will certainly fall. The choice is mine alone. If I wait too long, my lack of strength will make the choice for me. It's true; weakness makes a coward of us all. I choose to climb. Cautiously, I remove my left hand from the crack to put some chalk on it so I can get a better grip when I make my attempt. I get that hold back and chalk up my right hand. Then I swing that arm as far as I can over the ledge, searching for a crack, a minor indentation, a bump. Nothing. Nowhere.

I will myself to stretch farther, to become longer. Finding another centimeter, I search the rock again. There it is! I've got a hold! I move my legs as far up under the overhang as they can go. I release my left hand and arch it blindly over the rock to find another hold. My feet swing out. I squeeze and pull with all my strength. An abyss of nothingness lies below. There is nothing but air under me now.

Even though I've made that move, I'm still not safe. I make a transition in my moves from sheer strength to delicate placement. I slow my breathing to a more controlled level. To keep the monster within at bay, I maintain a calm mind and stay focused. From my tenuous position, I balance and move my left leg up and over the edge, and then I place my toe into a splinter of rock. It's not much, but it's just enough to pull myself from gravity's clutches. I reach safety, pausing for a moment to savor the victory. For this day I have overcome the monster and made the crux move!

2. Crux Moves in Life

On every climb there is a crux move, the single most difficult move on the climb. It's the point of no return. You either make the move or not. It's very much like the risks you have to take in life to reach your goals. The premise and the irony are the same: You have to let go of where you are at to make your move. You must take risks to be safe.

3. Crux Moves Journal

Insights	*Actions*

Insights	Actions

Insights	Actions

Why?

"If you have any doubts that we live in a society controlled by men, try reading down the index of contributors to a volume of quotations, looking for women's names."

—Elaine Gill

4. Why a Book on IntelligentRisking?

IntelligentRisking Cycle

No mountains can be climbed, no hearts won, and no victories found without risk. Some see risk as an opportunity to be avoided; however, the reality is that risk is an unavoidable opportunity. Since each of us faces risk every day the key is to learn to recognize which risks to take and how to take them in the smartest way possible. IntelligentRisking is how we set ourselves up for success.

As you attempt new things, you find new talents. As you find new talents, you discover greater success. With greater successes, your confidence builds. As you become more confident, you're willing to risk trying new things. This, in essence, is the IntelligentRisking cycle. The reality of IntelligentRisking is that if you choose the right risk and you take it in the smartest way possible, even if that risk doesn't turn out as planned it usually still turns out.

Every one of us has hopes, talents, and dreams that require us to risk. Deep inside we want to make a difference, not just in our own lives but also in the lives of others. Just as we want to give more, we want more out of life. IntelligentRisking is the term I use to describe how to take the right risks in life — how to create the meaningful life you want. Success is hard-won victories achieved by ordinary people taking one risk at a time toward their goal.

"Far better it is to dare mighty things, to win glorious triumphs, even though checkered by failure, than to take rank with those poor spirits who neither enjoy much nor suffer much, because they live in the gray twilight that knows not victory nor defeat."
—Teddy Roosevelt

5. Why IntelligentRisking for Women?

Even smart, talented and savvy women, fully capable of taking a higher level of risk, tend to hold back. This book explores what stops us and how we can effectively take those personal and professional risks that will make a difference in our lives.

Women tend to look at and react to risk differently from men. A round-up of recent research regarding the gender gap finds: Women's stress hormones and blood pressure tend to remain elevated at day's end; men's diminish after work. Eighty-five percent of working moms said they felt guilty about combining work and family (compared to 0% of working dads). Many of these differences are attributed to women trying to juggle their multiple and demanding roles — as spouse, mother, housekeeper, caretaker, employee and friend.[1]

Additionally, in 2002, women still held only 8% of the top executive positions in corporate America, including companies where the CEO is female.[2] The fact that women have not made more progress is amazing considering that women control about 80% of household spending and, using their own resources, makes up 46% of investors. Women buy 81% of all products and services, buy 75% of all over-the-counter medications, and make 82% of all grocery purchases. Forty percent of all business travelers are women. We head 40% of all U.S. households with annual incomes over $60,000. Yet, the wage gap between male and female managers actually widened between 1995 and 2000.[3]

That women are still struggling to find success in a traditional business environment is aptly expressed by the fact that 22% of all women with professional degrees including MBAs, MDs, and PhDs are not in the labor market.[4] The percentage of women working at least fifty hours a week is now higher in the United

States than in any other country in the world.[5] Looking for success outside of the traditional corporate environment women own roughly 66 percent of all home-based businesses.[6]

Women want to contribute in an effective and meaningful way without losing ourselves. We know we're bright enough. We know we have the education. We know we have the tools we need. We certainly work hard enough. So, what is keeping us from achieving the kind of success we desire?

The reality is that even though women are natural leaders, we are often reluctant to take the risks necessary for personal and professional success. I've seen this from many different perspectives during my thirty-three-year career. For the past ten years I've researched why so many bright, talented women shy away from taking risks that they want to take and are fully capable of implementing successfully.

Although I arrived at no simple answers after doing extensive quantitative and qualitative research, what I have uncovered is a unique phenomenon takes place within women. We know intellectually that we are very talented and skilled, and we want others to value our strengths and success. Yet, too often, we are the ones who ignore our strengths, play down our successes, focus on our mistakes, devalue our own accomplishments, and refuse to give ourselves the credit we've earned.

One key to IntelligentRisking is self-confidence, because no one can predict the course or outcome of a risk. That means that to risk, you must have a significant amount of confidence

1. How To Be Stress-Resiliant by Sara Brzowsky, published in Parade, October 12, 2003.
2. USA Today, January 27, 2003.
3. The Female CEO ca. 2002, by Margaret Heffernan, published in FASTCOMPANY.
4. Executive Women and the Myth of Having It All, by Sylvia Ann Hewlett
5. Ibid.
6. The Female CEO ca. 2002, by Margaret Heffernan, published in FASTCOMPANY.

and be willing to trust your own ability and resourcefulness to see the risk through-no matter what.

The irony is that women have what they need to risk, and yet it is difficult to hold on to the self-confidence we require if we continually underplay our successes, devalue our accomplishments, and sell ourselves short. These tendencies create a phenomenon where women who have the talent, the skill and the courage to risk hold back because they can't see their own potential. This book was created to help women awaken the leader within and start taking those risks that will make a positive difference.

It's Never Too Late

Why write this book now? Because it really is never too late to take a risk. Nancy Wells Hamilton is a partner in the litigation section of the Jackson Walker law firm in Houston, Texas. Her expertise is in complex commercial cases, intellectual property and First Amendment law. Nancy along with her partner, Chip Babcock, represented Oprah Winfrey during the famous Texas Cattlemen Beef Case in Amarillo, Texas in 1998. Chip was the lead attorney and Nancy held the second chair sitting next to Oprah during the six week trial. The case was won with a jury verdict in unfriendly cattle country.

Nancy initially started law school in the fall of 1980 in Chicago, Illinois at Chicago-Kent College of Law. Then Nancy met the man of her dreams, agreed to get married and moved with him to Houston, Texas. She transferred into the University of Houston Law School in 1981 and was scheduled to finish her degree in 1983.

Life however had other plans for Nancy, and she had a baby girl in April 1983, interrupting her final semester. She tried going back to school to finish up; however, with no family or friends in

Texas for support she decided to put her family first and take a leave of absence from school. Things didn't go as planned and in 1987 she found herself working part-time at an equestrian center for $5.00/hour and separated from her husband. During her divorce she was asked to explain why she never finished law school. Nancy knew it was too late to go back to school because they would never readmit her after a six year absence. She tried to explain that too much time had passed and she would simply not be allowed back in. The lawyers wouldn't take her word for it and asked for verification from the law school.

Nancy went to the school and asked them to confirm that she would not be readmitted. But the Dean would not provide a letter unless Nancy, first, formally petitioned for re-admission. Frustrated and only needing a simple "No" she wrote out in long hand on a legal pad her formal request for re-admittance to the law school explaining how her goals and priorities had changed and then changed back again. When she submitted her petition they informed her that she would be allowed to address the committee. This was an opportunity which seemed to be overkill for a simple "No" so she declined. She forgot about the whole thing and waited for the letter that would confirm what she already knew.

The letter never came. Instead, she got a phone call from the Dean informing her that the committee had met and on the basis of her petition she would be readmitted. Stunned and speechless she wondered how in the world she was going to deal with going back to law school after a six year absence. Unconvinced that she would be able to manage it all she asked the school if she could return on a part-time basis. This time she got her "No". It seemed they were a little worried over the length of time it was taking her to finish her degree.

Divorce so often seems like the end of the world, a risk that didn't work out and yet it also provides a new start with new opportunities. Clearly life was telling Nancy that it wasn't too late and she was supposed to take the risk of going back to law school. Accepting her fate and deciding that there was no real mystery to being an attorney she told herself, "I can figure this out." She jumped back into school and in 1989, nine years from when she started, Nancy graduated with a law degree, joined Jackson Walker and went on to successfully represent many high profile clients including one of today's most respected women, Oprah.

Need more proof? Grandma Moses, in her 70's began painting for her own enjoyment only because her arthritis made it too difficult to continue her embroidery and needlework. Louise Arner Boyd became the first woman to fly over the North Pole at the age of 67. Lillian Carter, mother of President Jimmy Carter, joined the Peace Corps and served for two years in India at the age of 68. Clara Barton, founder of the American Red Cross, rode mule wagons and worked as a nurse during the Spanish-American War at the age of 76. Eleanor of Aquitaine led an army to crush a rebellion against her son, King John of England at the age of 78. At the age of 71, Jenny Wood-Allen ran her first marathon and at 90, she completed the London Marathon in 11 hours and 34 minutes.

The moral of the story... it's never too late to become who you want to be.

Some Key Differences

My focus in this book is on women and what it takes to set yourself up for success by helping you see and live up to your potential. Even though men and women may have the same goal, our approaches and perspectives are quite different. To be successful it's important to understand some of these key differences.

My sixteen-year-old son, Connor, decided that he wanted a job, so he started picking up employment applications. Most of them asked for his qualifications and coming up with this list was not a problem. He thought he might get an interview so I asked him if he wanted to practice his interviewing skills, and he thought that might be a good idea. When I asked him why I might want to hire him, he answered with a list of qualities including that he was responsible, resourceful, hard working, and reliable. (Traits he was obviously saving up for his job.)

When I asked him why I might not want to hire him, he paused. Not just for a second but for a minute or two. Finally he asked what I meant. So I explained that some interviewers might ask him what he thought his weaknesses were. Being completely serious, he said that he didn't think he had any. Then he asked me what I thought. I have never had to bite my tongue harder! After some deliberation, I carefully mentioned that he has a very specific way of doing some things. He decided I was right and that his weakness was that he was too perfect. Do I need to say any more?

Most men tend to focus on their strengths, hide their weaknesses, play up their successes, place a high value on their accomplishments, take credit for positive outcomes and relax at the end of a hard day. If we women were to take a tip from the men, we could learn much that would benefit us in our careers and lives in general. The last section in this book is "Best Practices," which explores in greater detail the what, why, and how behind our gender differences in regard to risk taking.

The reality is that women already have what it takes to be successful risk takers. All we need is to be clear about what we want, focus on our strengths, and take intelligent risks to get there.

6. Why? Journal

Insights	Actions

Why?

Insights	Actions

Insights	Actions

IntelligentRisking

"Life is either a daring adventure or nothing at all."

—*Helen Keller*

7. The Art of Simplicity

In this era of information overload it's easy to make the simple complex, but the real trick is in making the complex simple. It took me one year to write this book on IntelligentRisking and four years to simplify it. The beauty in the IntelligentRisking process is that it's simple enough to use as a quick reference, and yet it provides you with the ability to add the depth and complexity you need for taking bigger risks.

Taking risks can be a very complicated and convoluted process. Depending on the risk, it might appear as if there are hundreds of things to consider and endless research and information that needs to be acquired before you can act. You may feel you need to speak with various experts ranging from accountants to project managers and from bankers to futurists. However, the reality is with limited time and multiple priorities that we need a quick and straightforward way to evaluate our options.

Countless books have been written on the subject of risk management, but very few focus on personal leadership, women, and risk. The books I have found always seem to lose me in a mass of background information, projections, and theories. I've searched for a book that would be relatively straightforward on the subject of risk, a book that would distill what I needed down into a manageable tool that would both remind me and help me to sort through some of the critical issues. Finding neither a book nor process that fit the bill, I decided to develop my own.

As a journal, this book will help you record your thoughts, insights, and actions. I'm convinced that the more involved we become in any process, the greater success we find. The simple act of writing down an idea will help embed it into our memory. Look at it as customizing this book for yourself, and use it as a valuable tool.

8. IntelligentRisking Definition

IntelligentRisking (in tel' e jent risk ing) **n .** An attitude, philosophy, and process that will help you choose which risks to take, when to take them, and how to see them through in the smartest way possible. IntelligentRisking will increase your probability for achievement by helping you maximize the odds for success while reducing the odds for a loss. IntelligentRisking is not a mysterious talent that some have and some don't; it's a real-world approach that appeals to your common sense. It's an art that's developed over a lifetime.

SYNONYMS: Astuteness, Confidence, Awareness, Courage, Determination, Thoughtfulness, Purposefulness, Commitment Premeditation, Resourcefulness, Intuition, Optimism, Pro-action, Wisdom, Assertiveness, Information and Inspiration.

Information and Inspiration Blended with Action

Have you ever wanted to lose ten pounds? Most of us have. Unless you have a rare medical condition, there are only two ways to lose weight: Eat less or exercise more; or better yet, do both. We all know it isn't the information that we're missing that keeps us from losing weight. It's the inspiration. That's why there are at least one hundred diet books on bookstore shelves at any given time. Why? We want to hear that there is an easier way. Some of my personal favorites are *How to Eat Everything You Want and*

Still Lose Weight and *How to Look Great without Exercising.* The reality is that you can have all the information and inspiration in the world and unless you act, nothing will change.

> *"Even if you're on the right track,*
> *you'll get run over if you just sit there."*
> —*Will Rogers*

The same is true with risk. There is so much information out there today that whether you decide to take the risk or not, you can find enough data to prove you are right. So, it's often not the information that helps us decide our course of action, it's the inspiration. Choosing to take a risk usually comes down to how much you want to achieve your goal. The information is what allows us to be smart about it. Yet, the key is still in taking action.

9. IntelligentRisking Premise

Most of us either don't take enough risk
or don't risk in smart enough ways.

Why? It's human nature to want to feel comfortable, safe, and in control. Risk by its very definition makes us feel uncomfortable, insecure, and out of control. The difficulty in taking a significant risk is that it creates a direct and unavoidable internal conflict. This conflict is exaggerated by another aspect of our human nature: our tendency to doubt ourselves too quickly, even though we know we have more strengths, talents, and skills than we are using.

This combination often starts a domino effect. We question ourselves. Internal alarms go off warning us that we may not have what it takes. We hesitate, and in our hesitation we allow fear, anger and ego to slip in; if we don't regain balance quickly, we can become lost, which reinforces our belief that we don't have what it takes. This undermines our true abilities and causes us to underestimate ourselves. This domino effect most often results in our giving up and quitting too soon.

Risk is the perceived difference between your evaluation of how difficult the challenge is and the perception you have of your own abilities. If you underestimate yourself and your abilities, then it stands to reason that you are overestimating the risk.

The Edge of Preconceived Limits

Great leaders are comfortable being uncomfortable.

When you start a project and begin feeling uncomfortable and insecure, it may not be because you lack the ability. It may be that you are simply nearing the edge of your preconceived limits. If so, your self-doubts are coming too early in the game and may not be valid. Your doubts can create a false sense of danger, causing you to unnecessarily question yourself, lose your courage, and give up too soon.

With IntelligentRisking you can begin to understand how to become comfortable with being uncomfortable. You will acquire the inspiration and the information required to transform your once-in-a-lifetime opportunities into once-in-a-lifetime successes. Keep in mind that IntelligentRisking is a dynamic process rather than a linear process. It is constantly evolving along with the new information and wisdom you are acquiring.

Past Victories

Now, please think of a risk that you are proud that you took. It doesn't necessarily have to be one that turned out just the way you planned (they rarely do, anyway). It could be anything-for example, it could be saying "no" to that job, or saying "yes" to that job; going back to school, or dropping out. What the risk was doesn't matter as much as why you're proud that you took it. Take a moment to really think about that risk; you may want to make some notes about it on the journaling pages provided.

What you just did is a very important component of IntelligentRisking for women. You visualized yourself as a successful risk taker. The more you see and believe that you are good at taking risks, the more likely you'll risk successfully in the future.

Tackling a new challenge always involves some risk. The larger the challenge, the more significant the risk — it is easy to begin to feel confused and overwhelmed. It's hard to know where to start, it's difficult to find the right path, and it's easy to doubt yourself. In the past you may have been too afraid to start, too timid to be effective, or too unsure to see it through. There were probably times when it seemed easier to do nothing rather than risk making a mistake. The end result may have been letting an opportunity slip through your fingers, only to regret it later.

10. Mountain Analogy

Each of us faces challenges and goals with associated risks.
They are the mountains we must climb.

By using a mountain analogy, you can make a valuable shift in your perspective about risk. This, in turn, will help you internalize your own challenges in a new way, creating a powerful visual parallel to your own goals. You will find that you can simplify things professionally or personally by asking questions such as "What is the real mountain here?" and "What mountain am I climbing?"

When climbing a technical route on an actual mountain, you climb one pitch (or rope length) at a time. The bigger the mountain, the more pitches required. The truth is, if you can climb one pitch, you can climb a mountain.

The most important climb is the one you are on at the moment. Doing well on this mountain is what will determine your forward progress. There will always be others who take more difficult routes. There will always be those around you climbing more dangerous mountains. Your focus can't be on them. At any point in time you may be able to look backward or forward and see other mountains that may seem more important in comparison. Yet, the mountain you are climbing today is the only one that truly matters right now.

"Climbing Mt. Everest is basically a challenge between the individual and themselves and the individual and their mountain. In life, we are all climbing a mountain like Everest and the key to success is much the same. It's not the mountain we conquer, it's ourselves."

—Sir Edmund Hillary

11. IntelligentRisking Concepts and Strategies

This book explores two key concepts of IntelligentRisking-Invisible Risk and the Courage Ratio — as well as the four IntelligentRisking strategies: **Choose Your Mountain**, **Plan Your Route**, **Build Your Courage**, and **Climb Strong!** It concludes with a review of "The 12 Critical IntelligentRisking Questions" every woman should ask before taking a risk. There are numerous journal pages throughout the book designed for you to capture your insights and commit to action.

12. An Attitude, Philosophy and Process

IntelligentRisking is the art of turning mountains into molehills.

IntelligentRisking Components

IntelligentRisking is an attitude and a philosophy as much as it is a process. It creates an intellectual atmosphere in which you look at your situation from multiple perspectives, understand how you may be filtering information, determine a proactive approach, and finally transform your inspiration and information into dynamic action. We will take a quick look at each of these four components or abilities:

1. View risk from multiple perspectives.
2. Identify how you filter information.

3. Take a proactive approach.

4. Transform inspiration and information into dynamic action.

13. The Medicine Wheel

Risk is a Matter of Perspective

IntelligentRisking means looking at the whole picture from multiple angles. The more points of view you are able to consider, the better decision you'll make. Some challenges are more personal in nature while others are more professional. However, there are few professional risks that don't impact us personally, just as there are few personal risks that don't touch our lives professionally.

Some American Indian tribes use a medicine wheel to look at their challenges from multiple perspectives. They draw a circle in the dirt and place stones around the circle's edge. Each stone represents a different point of view. With great ceremony the medicine man places a single eagle's feather in the center of the circle. The feather represents the issue they are facing, and it is looked at from the angle of each stone. Naturally, the perspective changes along with the line of sight. One perspective offers only the sharp edge of the feather, another offers light, and a third, only darkness.

Risk or Opportunity?

A great friend of mine who has brainstormed many of these concepts with me for hours on end is Brian O'Malley. As a police officer, Brian carried a skateboard painted to match his patrol car.

This was over 15 years ago and the kids on his beat thought it was cool. It wasn't long before word got out to the captain that O'Malley was using a new set of unauthorized wheels. He remembers the afternoon the captain called him in and told him he could no longer ride his skateboard with the kids because it was too dangerous. To this day he wonders how they could they expect him to be a street cop and a member of the S.W.A.T. team and then forbid him to ride his skateboard because it was too risky.

Consider this: For every risk you would not consider, is there someone else out there doing it right now? An avid day trader may be highly successful behind a computer screen yet terrified to speak in front of a group. A gambler might head to Las Vegas with thousands of dollars but would never consider investing in a high-risk technology stock. A college student might not hesitate to leap out of an airplane to skydive, but be afraid to approach a stranger to ask for a date.

People and organizations can be quite odd in the way they look at risk. They worry about plane crashes that kill 200 people a year, yet don't think twice about car accidents that kill more than 40,000 a year. Some people worry about being killed by flesh-eating bacteria (chances: 1 in 1 million), AIDS contracted from a blood transfusion (1 in 96,000), or lightening strikes (1 in 30,000). Yet, in truth, one out of ten premature deaths are linked to the following six common behaviors: smoking cigarettes, overeating, misusing alcohol, failing to control high blood pressure, not exercising, and not wearing seat belts in cars.

The same person who says rock climbing is too dangerous might not think twice about getting behind the wheel after a drink or two. Most people think nothing of driving on a two-lane highway with another vehicle headed toward them in another lane at 60 m.p.h. You may be a good driver, yet what about that other guy? You'll be passing within a few feet of each other. A two-second slip in concentration can result in complete devastation. It happens hundreds of times each day. What one person considers an unacceptable risk another jumps in without hesitation.

14. The Myth of Objectivity

Identifying How You Filter Information

Clearly we all look at risk differently. Let's explore why. Facts provide the objective information. Yet the facts mean little out of context. Context is created out of our subjectivity. Depending on whose context you use, the meaning can vary dramatically.

All of us have gone out in search of information. We often use the information that supports our view and dismiss any information that doesn't. No disrespect intended, politicians have turned 'the spin' into an art. They have refined it to such a point that they don't even have to go out and find the right set of facts; they've become so skilled that they can actually use the same facts to argue both sides. Many of us have become increasingly savvy about not believing all we hear from others. The question is, do you put your own opinions through such scrutiny?

**If facts mean little out of context,
then let the context begin.**

You wake up to a freak ice storm. Every news channel is repeating warnings not to drive. Most of the main roads have been closed, and there are travel advisories out for the ones still open. Do you go to work? Of course not! You aren't going to risk being in an accident for work.

So you settle down into a comfortable chair with a great book since your passion is reading. The weather continues to worsen throughout the day. You start wondering if tonight's book auction, which you've looked forward to for months, will be canceled. You desperately want that rare book, and you must be there in person to bid. All of a sudden the roads are looking better. Didn't that announcer just say, "If you go out, be careful"? That must mean the roads are getting clearer. Maybe you could make it. No one else is going to be out driving in this storm, so that would make it even safer.

You begin to hear the information a little differently based on your own interests. We all do it. It's human nature. However, if you are willing to recognize that your passion for books may be distorting the way you are looking at the storm, then you may think twice before going out. If you are unaware, or if you choose to ignore how your passion and interests are filtering the conditions, and go out anyway then you'll be taking a careless chance versus an Intelligent Risk.

The danger doesn't lie in "not" being objective. The danger lies in thinking that you are being objective when you aren't.

Subjectively Objective

IntelligentRisking doesn't require you to be totally objective; just the contrary; it asks you to recognize that you are, like all of us, subjectively objective. You are probably aware of this, yet like all of us, you may try to kid yourself or others by saying things like, "I'm being completely objective about this." If you ever catch yourself saying or thinking this, beware. You are setting yourself up to take an uninformed risk. To dramatically increase your chances of risking success-fully begin asking yourself, "I know I'm being subjective. How I'm filtering this information?"

15. Proactive vs. Reactive

*If you aren't choosing your own risks,
someone else will be choosing them for you.*

Taking a Proactive Approach

Success requires that, as often as possible, you make your own choices. In my IntelligentRisking programs I hear example after example from people who listened to others and followed the wrong path because they didn't have the courage to forge their own trail. I have met accountants who wanted to be artists, artists who wanted to teach, teachers who wanted to be attor-neys, and attorneys who wanted to be accountants. Each person is different, yet their stories are the same. They all regret not climbing their own mountain.

IntelligentRisking is a dynamic process, and it requires you to be proactive. It means if you don't like the direction things are headed, it's your job to set a new heading. If you aren't happy not making any interest on your money, you need to pull it out of the mattress and invest it. If you think your life is boring, then you are boring. It's your responsibility to make your own life exciting.

Accept, Reject, or Change

Climbing Mt. Everest is an excellent example of how valuable it is for a person to adapt to harsh conditions. It's an asset because you find new levels of endurance, stamina, and hopefully performance. If you haven't attempted climbing the real Mt. Everest, then perhaps you've experienced this to a lesser degree at some time in your own life.

However, there are times when learning to adapt to severe conditions is a serious liability. Adapting to an extremely harsh, negative environment should be treated as a temporary challenge. It should be a situation that you get through, become a better person from, and then move on. It should not be accepted as the norm. Too often we find ourselves adapting to and trapped inside difficult environments in our everyday lives. If you are stuck in an abusive relationship or reporting to a boss who harasses you then you need to take the risk of getting out.

If you're unhappy in your job, don't wait around only to act surprised when you're offered early retirement at the age of thirty-one. When things aren't working, whether it's personally or professionally, you essentially have three choices: *Accept, Change,* or *Reject.*

If your specific situation is not working, it's your responsibility to acknowledge what is happening and make a choice. You may choose to *Accept* it because it really isn't that bad. You may decide to *Change* it and fix the problems because you want it to work. Or you may decide to *Reject* the situation and leave on your own terms.

Each decision involves different kinds of challenges and risks. Any one of these choices may be the "right" choice for varying reasons. IntelligentRisking means that you don't take a risk out of default. Instead you make a thoughtful, deliberate, and conscious choice about what course of action will be best.

16. Dynamic Action

Blending Information and Inspiration

When you contemplate a risky venture, you need to explore two components: information and inspiration. You may have been taught, over the course of a lifetime, that all risks can be measured. Although many pieces of the puzzle can be quantified, no one has yet figured out how to measure all aspects of a risk. If everything could be measured and calculated then it wouldn't really be a risk. Acquiring the information you need to make smart choices is critically important. If you are taking the risk of buying a new home and trying to decide between two different types of home loans, what you will need the most is accurate information.

However, in most cases the challenge you are considering simply isn't black and white. Information alone is not adequate. It is important to consider other factors and recognize that the inspiration you have is equally important. In fact, it can often determine the outcome.

Inspiration is what will see you through.

For every challenge you find overwhelming, you don't have to look far to find inspiration from others. I found a visual example of this one day when I took my boys to the skateboard park. Kids at every skill level raced around in all possible directions at every imaginable speed. Some were on skateboards, others on roller blades, and a few on BMX trick bikes. At first I thought, "This is insane. They're all going to crash." Then as I studied the chaos it was clear each kid had his own place in the system. There was a rhythm to the madness that the kids seemed to understand. What was the common denominator? Passion.

For every skater who looked like a beginner, there was another who knew even less. For every skater I thought was the best, there was one next to him doing an even more difficult stunt. Each kid out there was, at the same time, both a student and teacher to those around them. One minute I'd see one of the experienced skaters giving advice to a little kid. The next minute when that "expert" lost a bet with Newton's Law of Gravity, it was the little kid handing out the advice and encouragement.

It was easy to see which ones already knew about IntelligentRisking. They were the ones with the helmets and pads. It was also interesting to see the culture they created around "getting tough." If any one of those kids took a hard fall at home, they'd have limped inside to Mom with a couple tears and get tons of sympathy. Out here though, there's a different expectation: If you're seriously hurt, we'll help, otherwise... stop whining.

Every skater out there was missing tricks, taking falls, and getting scraped up. It was at times hard to watch. No doubt the paramedics make regular stops there. Yet, I overheard the kids saying some interesting things to each other, like "Start with some easy stuff and keep your balance. Everybody falls, just get back up." Good advice for any endeavor. Despite all their mishaps, one fact remained obvious. Those without passion leave. Those with passion pick themselves up and try again.

17. The Risk of Complacency

Did You Take More Risks When You Were Younger?

We all start out with an inherently adventurous spirit, yet too often that spirit fades over time. Each of us faces the danger of getting too comfortable and becoming too complacent with our lives. Each of us, when not pushed, sets comfortable, artificial limits for ourselves.

Chances are that when you were younger you were more willing to try new things and take more risks. We all understand how important this is that's why parents go out of their way to give children the opportunity to explore new interests so that they can find hidden talents. The question is, do you do this for yourself? Isn't it just as important for you to continue to explore new interests and uncover hidden talents so that you can continue to grow?

We all need a push.

One of the fastest growing industries in the United States is personal training. Personal trainers are great for setting up exercise programs that are both safe and effective. Unfortunately, many of us become reliant on a personal trainer to push us. We depend on them to tell us to do "one more push-up." Now, we all know we should do one more push-up. It's just that without their inspiration and motivation we won't do that "one more" on our own. Why? Because we like to be comfortable and that last one is hard to do, yet we know it's the most valuable one. Only by going beyond our "limit" do we build.

18. IntelligentRisking Journal

Insights	*Actions*

Insights	Actions

The Courage Ratio

"One isn't necessarily born with courage, but one is born with potential. Without courage, we cannot practice any other virtue with consistency. We can't be kind, true, merciful, generous, or honest."
—*Maya Angelou*

19. The Courage Ratio

The Jump

Imagine you are walking along one of the beautiful beaches in Acapulco. In the distance you can see the cliff divers performing their incredible swan dives from a one-hundred-foot ledge. You're thinking, "Wow, that looks like so much fun... for them."

You continue on and are now standing on a rock that's just barely sticking up out of the water. The ocean is perfectly clear and warm. You're an excellent swimmer. There are no sharks, not like yesterday. The sun is high and you're getting hot.

This is the scenario I present in my programs. Then I ask the audience to participate. As you read on, consider how you might react. "Raise your hand if you would be willing to dip your toes into the water to cool off." (At this point everyone's hand is raised.) "Would you be willing to jump into the water from one foot? If so raise your hand and keep your hand up until you personally would-n't be willing to jump." "Would you be willing to jump in from five feet up?" "Ten feet?" (Some of the hands are going down.) "Fifty feet?" (Most of the hands are down.) "Would you be willing to jump just once from one hundred feet?" (All but one or two hands are down.)

This is a straightforward example of a risk/reward ratio. As the audience sees the risk go up in relationship to the reward, their hands go down. Now, what if we changed the equation slightly? "Would you consider jumping *just once* from one hundred feet for one million dollars cash, tax-free?" Before I can finish saying "tax free" most of the hands are in the air. Many are saying, "Just show me where." However, others are still saying, "No way." Which group would you be in?

Let's change the equation again. "What if I told you that some-one you loved more than anyone else in this world was dying and needed an operation that cost one million dollars to save his or her life?" Would you be willing to jump?

Most of the people who had still been unwilling to jump change their minds at this point. Within seconds the entire audience has shifted from "No way, I won't jump" to "Sure I'll jump, just show me where." **Did the risk of getting hurt ever change? No.** The risk of injury was exactly the same seconds ago as it is right now. **What changed? Your passion.**

Behind every risk is a fear. Behind every reward is a passion. When your passion is greater than your fear, you find your courage.

The Courage Ratio:
Passion > Fear = Courage

The Courage Ratio takes the risk/reward ratio to the next level by exploring the true motivators that lie underneath our behavior. For every risk you're afraid to take, is there someone else out there doing it? Probably. Why would that risk be acceptable to them yet not to you? Some of the questions you might want to ask yourself are, "What's my problem with this risk? What's my fear behind the risk? Why is this reward so meaningful to me? What's the passion that this reward taps into for me?"

20. Signature Risks

Hallmark Cards

All of us have "signature risks," those experiences that have defined us in a unique way. One of mine took place while I worked at Hallmark Cards. My degree was in industrial design from the University of Illinois, and my first job was working in the field designing stores for Hallmark Cards. After a few years I was promoted to assistant product manager and transferred into the home office in Kansas City. My job then was to get Hallmark into the gift business. Since all the stores are privately owned and not franchised, the shops could and did buy their gift items from other vendors.

It was an obvious mountain, and the route was also clear. The existing product managers of the various product lines would develop gifts for the program. Even though I was close to the bottom of the Hallmark food chain, I met with all the product managers, who agreed to design gifts for the program. Important to note is that none of the product managers reported to me, the gift program was not part of their goals, and it would require a ton of extra work for them. What did they do? The same thing you and I would have done in their place. They met their own goals, and the gift program waited.

The first year I got a couple of votive candles and not much more. The second year was promising similar results, so I went to my boss and asked for help, direction, guidance. I still have not forgotten that day twenty-plus years ago when he looked me right in the eye and said, "Barbara, if I need to help you then I don't need you, do I?"

You can imagine what I was thinking as I walked out of his office. I'd be lying if I told you I wasn't furious and scared. This was my first real close up look at the risk/reward ratio and my own fears and passions. My fear was that of being set up and possibly fired. My passion was to prove I could do it (without any help from my boss). I had a choice to make: Be a victim or fight back. I chose to fight, and that was a defining moment in my life.

I decided that as my own risk/reward ratio had changed, I would have to find a way to do the same for the product managers. I realized that I needed some leverage. Why not start at the top? I called Don Hall (as in the Hall family who own Hallmark), or at least I called his secretary, who had absolutely no idea who I was. I told her I was setting up an important meeting to launch Hallmark into the gift business and it was critical that Don Hall attend. This was back in the days of paper and pencil calendars. She asked me when, and I asked her what would work for Mr. Hall. She gave me a date! I now had some leverage.

My next calls were to the other senior executive's offices. I explained to their secretaries that I was setting up a meeting to launch Hallmark into the gift business but I wasn't sure if their bosses should attend; however, Don Hall would be there. Of course they all thought their bosses should be there too. I now had a meeting scheduled with every senior executive throughout Hallmark Cards.

Next I wrote a letter to the product managers. I thanked them for all of their support and said that I was looking forward to seeing the products they'd been developing. I also told them that if for any reason they couldn't deliver products again this year not to worry, I'd already set up a meeting to discuss the obstacles keeping Hallmark out of this multimillion-dollar market. I attached a list of attendees. The Hallmark Gift Program was launched.

My passion overrode my fears, and I found the courage to act. I discovered a greater level of resourcefulness, confidence, and assertiveness within myself than I had ever dreamed existed. If I hadn't taken that risk I'm not sure what would have happened. Chances are I wouldn't have been fired, but I would have been stripped of my pride. Because of that risk I found the courage to follow a dream, to leave Hallmark and go to work for Walt Disney.

If you find yourself with a challenge, a goal, or a dream that you want to follow but lack the courage, then look beyond the risks and rewards. Uncover your fears and passions so that you can find the courage to act.

21. Courage Ratio Journal

Insights	Actions

Insights	Actions

Invisible Risk

"Failure is impossible."
—Susan B. Anthony

22. Playing It Too Safe

Some of you during the jump scenario might have been thinking, "Hey, wait a minute, you changed the whole deal." Yes, I did. Chances are your initial focus was based on what would happen if you took the risk. When I introduced a loved one who was dying, chances are your focus shifted to what would happen if you didn't take the risk. You saw the Invisible Risk of not acting. Invisible Risk is the risk we take when we try to play it too safe. It's the regret of not pursuing our talents, hopes, and dreams.

How About a Risk-Free Life?

At times, the challenges may just seem too hard and you wish you could have a risk-free life. Some people say, "I'm not a risk taker. I want to avoid risk at all costs." OK, let's consider what kind of life that would be. How would that change your day?

Maybe now you jog around the block, take a shower, drink coffee, and make toast before driving to work. You'd better cut out the jogging because you could twist your ankle. A lot of people fall in the shower, so don't go there. You might burn your tongue drinking coffee, so forget that. It's possible that you could shock yourself on the toaster or get in an accident on the road to work. Maybe you'd better just stay in bed. Oh no! You'd better not stay in bed; statistics show most people die lying in bed. That's right... there's no such thing as a risk-free life.

Three Most Common Types of Invisible Risk:
The Waiting Place
The Hiding Place
The Ghosts of Risks Past

23. The Waiting Place

*"Things that matter most must never be at
the mercy of things that matter least."*
—*Johann Wolfgang von Goethe*

Failure to Act

It's easy to get caught up in the Waiting Place. It happens when you find yourself wanting everything to be perfect, looking for a guarantee, wishing it were easy, or thinking you don't have enough time. However, when it comes to taking a risk you'll find that it's never perfect, there are no guarantees, it's seldom easy, and there is never enough time or information.

A woman came up to me after a program and confessed her need for perfection. Suzanne had been waiting for an assistant manager position to open up. By the time the job became available she wanted it so badly she could taste it. Her goal was to send the perfect resume with impeccable references. She wanted to take her time, so she thought she would write it over the weekend. Before she submitted it she wanted a few of her close friends to review it. Then, she decided to print it on nicer paper. Still dissatisfied, she decided to redo it. Suzanne didn't want to send it out until she confirmed the exact title of the recipient. She wanted to deliver it in person and decided to wait until she bought a new suit so she'd look her best. One month later, her resume still didn't look good enough, but she thought perhaps she should still drop it off. When she did she learned the position had just been filled. Her need to be perfect cost her the perfect job.

No Risk

We live in a society that encourages risk taking. Our country and many of our most successful businesses were founded in risk; yet recently we have seen a proliferation of "Risk-Free" promotions. Have you ever actually tried to return one of those "no-risk", money-back items? If you actually have the receipt and the original packing plus you have lots of time, patience, and tenacity, then you may actually get your money back (if the offer hasn't already expired).

There are few guarantees in this life, and if anyone tells you that you can take a risk guaranteed to work then you better turn to someone else for advice.

The time is now.

It's never too late to start, and it's best not to put off until tomorrow things that matter today. If you catch yourself thinking, "That's something I'd love to try if I were just a little bit younger." Then think again.

The Value of Time
To realize the value of one year,
ask a student who has failed a grade.

To realize the value of one month,
ask a mother who has given birth to a premature baby.

To realize the value of one week,
ask an editor of a weekly newspaper.

To realize the value of one day,
ask the person who filed his taxes on April 16th.

To realize the value of one minute,
ask the traveler who has just missed a plane.
To realize the value of one millisecond,
ask the athlete who just won a silver medal at the Olympics.

—Author unknown

Olympic Moment of Opportunity

An Olympic Moment of Opportunity is that brief window of time when your mental, emotional, and physical readiness coincides with a situation that together offers you a high potential for success.

It's not every day that circumstances will call upon your unique wisdom and experience. It's not every day that you feel fit and healthy. It's not every day you have the chance to help someone in trouble. It's not every day you can be a hero in your own adventure. Will you grab that once-in-a-lifetime opportunity and turn it into a once-in-a-lifetime success?

Regrets don't come from taking risks that failed.
Regrets come from failing to take risks.

How to Break Out of the Waiting Place:

If you are a perfectionist...
- Set deadlines.
- Trust that you'll do your best.
- Don't grant yourself unlimited extensions
  to get more information·
- Make a decision and take action.

If you are looking for a guarantee...
- Recognize there are no "true" guarantees.
- If you still feel you need a guarantee,
  then question if the risk is too high.
- Ask yourself if the guarantee is worth
  losing the opportunity over.

If you want it easier....
- While you are waiting for a genie to come along and wave
  his magic wand, just take one more step, then one more.

If you are a waiting for more time or the right time...

Since no one has invented a way to make more time, try these
ways to find the right time. When you hear yourself saying any
of the following phrases (as you put off doing something that
really matters), try a different approach. Change the way you
think and you'll change your life.

- I'll do it later ~ I'll do it this week
- I'm too busy ~ I'm simplifying my life
- I don't have the time ~ If it's important, I'll find the time
- I have no time for myself ~ I'm making time for myself
- I'll have time for this later ~ What can I change to create time now?
- My time just isn't my own ~ I'm in charge of my time
- I'd love to, but I'm too busy ~ Schedule it; I'll rearrange
  some things

24. The Hiding Place

"I had a lot of troubles in my life but most of them never happened."
—Mark Twain

Unwilling to Let Go

When you find your emphasis changing from "playing to win" to "playing not to lose," you know you have fallen into the Hiding Place. This Invisible Risk usually appears once you have achieved some measure of success. That's when we are more likely to shift from dynamic, proactive risk-taking into a static, reactive mode. When we are content, we sometimes create boundaries, patterns, habits, rules, assumptions, and paradigms to protect us. The risk here is that we might end up trapped by our efforts to remain content.

The status quo is a moving target.

In lieu of seeking to fulfill a dream or pursue a passion, you decide that life isn't so bad in this comfort zone. You've got it made. Why rock the boat? You'll camp here. Are you making a temporary camp? Or is it looking a little more permanent? Howard Hughes is an example of a person who built and controlled an empire. Then, in an effort to protect his success, he allowed his empire to control him.

Disney

The longer you stand still, the farther away you drift from your own desired goals. You don't have what you want, but you're afraid to move on, fearing that you'll lose what you do have. As hard as it is to let go, to move forward, you must.

Entrepreneurial companies that catapult to success with cutting-edge products and services can grow conservative and timid as they attempt to retain their position. I joined Disney just after Walt Disney had passed away and there was a distinct void in the leadership. The entire company had slipped into "if we change anything we'll lose what we have" mode.

No one dared to modernize the characters' looks. When I reached across the table to point out where we might want to put Mickey Mouse on a skateboard I thought I was going to have my hand slapped. The company had unknowingly slipped into a defensive posture to guard its position, forgetting the strategies and skills it had used to garner success in the first place.

Fortunately, I reported indirectly to a fabulous leader, Bo Boyd. Bo has a unique style that blends common sense, vision and political savvy. At the time he was a Vice President who later was promoted to President and then Chairman of Disney Consumer Products. He's given me valuable counsel over the years and become a life-long friend. When I worked at Disney I would turn to him for advice whenever I would hit one of these invisible walls within the company. I remember him telling me, "Barbara, always do the right thing and ask for forgiveness later." Great advice that I continue to use to this day.

The company was facing an Invisible Risk, it was trying not to change in a world that was changing. What happened? Michael Eisner happened... with a takeover and makeover resulting in phenomenal success and growth.

How to Leave the Hiding Place:

- Make sure you understand what it is you are trying to hold on to.
- Sit down and make a list of what it is you are trying to protect.
- Add to your list how much all this protection is costing you in time, energy, and money.
- Compare your lists, challenging each item for its validity. If you have more to lose than gain, you need to reconsider tak-

ing this risk. Ask yourself how you would feel if you quit. Ask yourself if you would have regrets.

- Challenge yourself by asking if you're spending more time, energy, and money worrying about doing it than it would take to actually do it.
- Now make two more lists. First a list of everything that you might "actually" lose. Second a list of everything you might "realistically" gain.
- Consider the worst-case scenario, then ask yourself if you could handle it.
- Rather than quit, perhaps you could find a way to take smaller steps minimizing potential losses.
- Recognize that if you are putting most of your energy into trying not to lose, then you are actually sabotaging your own efforts to win.
- Ask yourself if you are trying too hard to hang on to your comfort zone.
- Yesterday's status quo is not the same as it is today. In truth, the status quo is a moving target.

25. The Ghosts of Risks Past

"Everyone thought I was bold and fearless and
even arrogant, but inside I was always quaking."
—*Katharine Hepburn*

Lack of Self-confidence

The Ghosts of Risks Past are the memories of your own personal successes and failures. They can be a negative or a positive filter through which you view information and make judgments. These negative memories contribute to the voice of the Monster Within, that inner voice you hear when you begin to doubt yourself, your decisions, and your abilities. Your successful experiences create friendly ghosts that whisper encouragement, giving you the confidence to try again.

Women seldom over emphasize their successes in fact we do just the opposite. We tend to focus and over emphasize our mistakes and failures. Sometimes your failures will haunt you to the point that they make your memories of an actual incident worse than the reality. Failures can promote excessive caution. A previous lack of success can contribute to your fears and persuade you to avoid risk at any cost. These ghosts provoke the Monster Within.

The Ghosts of Risks Past certainly play a role in how you filter information. They can blur your view; they can dominate your thoughts; they can dictate your choices. Take a moment and do a quick scan of your "ghosts." Are they encouraging or discouraging? If they are friendly, then great, you have a solid foundation. If the ghosts are frightening, then look at them in the light of IntelligentRisking to learn from past risks and to reframe failed attempts as nothing more than stepping-stones to future successes. In this way you'll get back in control of them instead of them controlling you.

How to Tame the Ghosts of Risks Past:

- Avoid thinking or saying, "I'm not good enough." Replace that phrase with, "I'm getting better every day."

- Take an inventory of your strengths and accomplishments. Keep that list handy, and whenever possible, do things that play to your strengths.
- Build a strong support team that believes in you.
- If you're having a really tough day, call someone on your team and tell him or her, "Today is hard; I need a pep talk."
- Tune out pessimists.
- Drop anyone who consistently tells you in a critical way that you aren't good enough.
- Pay attention to when you hear the Monster Within. Is it in the evenings? When you're tired? After arguing with family or friends? If you know when you're most likely to hear the monster, it will be easier for you to ignore its whispers.
- If the monster is breathing down your neck, get away. Break the mood and go see a movie, go workout, read a book, or take a drive. Do something that makes you feel good and focuses your mind on something else.
- Look at the risk involved if you quit.
- Make a list of why you want to do this and refer back to it when you question yourself.
- Visualize your future success. Whether you actually draw it, or create it out of words, or cut pictures out of magazines, create a picture of you reaching your goal and keep it near by. Pull it out anytime it gets hard to carry on.

26. Invisible Risks

What If You Do? What If You Don't?

Searching for Invisible Risks allows you to increase your information base and broaden your perspective. This enables you to make the best decision possible with the information you have available at the time. Invisible Risks are only dangerous when we don't consider them in our decision making process. Question yourself daily about your decisions and examine how you filter information (subjective objectivity). As you climb your mountain, continue to ask every step of the way, "What if I do?" and "What if I don't?"

My friend Brian had the dramatic experience of being with others as they came to grips with their Invisible Risks during his twenty-plus years on the streets as a police officer and paramedic firefighter. He told me, "During this time I had the opportunity to be with people in the final moments of their lives. Those were powerful, powerful moments. The sad part was that so many people had regrets. Their regrets sounded like these: 'I wish I had pursued that dream. I wish I had said the things I wanted to say to the people that meant the most to me. I wish I had taken a chance on the talent that was inside me. No one else knew it was there, yet I knew and I didn't take the chance.' " Not all of us have those feelings of regret, yet far too many of us do.

Regrets are insidious because the question of
"what might have been" can haunt you forever.

Regrets have a way of accumulating over the years. They can creep up on you and ambush you from behind long after you thought you had gotten over them. They subconsciously undermine your confidence and erode your spirit.

Invisible Risk
If I try, I risk possible failure;
If I don't try, I risk certain failure.

If I change, I risk the unknown;
If I don't change, I risk being left behind.

If I believe in myself, I risk disappointment;
If I don't believe in myself, I risk not becoming all I can be.

If I climb, I risk falling;
If I don't climb, I risk never reaching the summit.

Frank Felt

I recently met the most extraordinary man. His name is Frank Felt. He has his Ph.D. in political science and was a senior analyst for the CIA. He was diagnosed with melanoma that spread into his lymph nodes. His doctors removed his lymph glands and determined there was nothing else left to do. It was too late for chemotherapy. Their advice? Quit your job and do whatever will make you happy. You probably only have six months left to live, at the most.

Frank did just that. He quit his job, sold his house, bought a motor home, and went off to do something that he had only dreamed about since he was six years old: Frank ran off and joined the circus.

Now you may be thinking, that's a great story and it is unusual, but what makes Frank extraordinary? Well, all of this happened to him twenty-four years ago, when he was forty-nine. Frank is now seventy-three and he's still with the circus. He went from assistant manager to running the circus on the road to ring master, and today he is still managing the advanced sales. Amazing, isn't it?

I asked Frank, "With all your wisdom and 20-20 hindsight, what do you think happened?" He said, "I had been fascinated by the circus since my father took me at the age of five. When I got out of the service it just didn't seem an appropriate choice for a career. How do you go home and tell your family you're joining a circus? That diagnosis was a gift. It gave me the freedom to follow my dream. When I did join the circus I never had to work so hard in my life, and I had never ever had so much fun. I just don't think I had time to be sick any more."

What Are Your Invisible Risks?

What Invisible Risks are out there for you? Is there an area in your life in which you're playing it too safe? Is there something out there that you want to do but feel it would be safer if you didn't take the risk? Looking at risks from multiple perspectives is imperative. However, it is difficult for many of us to see the potential loss or negative consequence that comes with inaction. Too often we believe that if we do nothing, we'll be safe. We have the misconception that if we can just ignore what's happening around us, we won't have to take any risks at all.

27. Invisible Rewards

Just as there are Invisible Risks, there are Invisible Rewards that can be equally difficult to see. If something doesn't turn out as you hoped it is often hard to see the value in the experience. With IntelligentRisking the Invisible Rewards are made up of the intangibles like the confidence and pride you walk away with when you know you did the right thing for the right reason. Invisible Rewards lie in the wisdom and insights you gain about yourself and how you will do things differently in the future. It is the depth of character and the empathy you acquire from the experience.

Heroes in Education

I did an IntelligentRisking program for Peggy McAllister, executive director of the New Hampshire Association of School Principals. One of the greatest things about what I do is that I get to meet so many amazing people and hear so many incredible stories. During the association's annual meeting they present the traditional Principal of the Year Award and also something very special: Heroes in Education Awards. The year I was speaking at their conference this honor was bestowed on a principal who had been pressured by his school board to fire one of his most outstanding teachers. The reason they wanted this teacher let go was not for any substantial reason—it came down to someone on the board having a personal conflict with the teacher. The principal refused based on his own principles, and he was subsequently relieved of his own job. He took the risk for the right reason: to protect a teacher from being wrongly dismissed. He definitely deserved the Heroes in Education award. It would be great if every organization offered a "Hero" award to emphasize the need and value of doing the right thing.

As I've said earlier in this book, if you take the right risk for the right reason in the smartest way possible, even if it doesn't turn out as hoped it still usually turns out. In addition to several invisible rewards, the principal mentioned previously received a more tangible reward: a job in a different district that ended up being a better job, with more money and an opportunity for him to work with a school district that shared his values. So often, risks taken for the right reason that don't turn out quite the way we hope lead to other, greater opportunities and more tangible rewards down the road.

28. Invisible Risk Journal

Insights	Actions

Insights	*Actions*

Choose Your Mountain

The mountains you chose yesterday have defined who you are today. The mountains you choose today will define who you will become tomorrow.

29. Why Choose a Mountain?

Honor and Respect

Many of you have probably faced bigger challenges and taken greater risks than have I. It's important to me that you know that I respect and honor all of you and the mountains you have climbed.

Compelling Future

We are all climbing a mountain in our lives, some literally and some figuratively. Having a clear goal creates a certain amount of synergy, which in turn translates into a tremendous level of focused energy. In truth, the challenge you decide to pursue creates a compelling future. It starts to define your choices and actions. George Burns set his sights on performing in the Palladium at the age of one hundred. He even sold tickets to the show. Although he didn't get to perform there on that date, he did celebrate his one-hundredth birthday. How did he live so long? He had created a very compelling future for himself.

You get what you focus on. If you choose to become a world-class ballet dancer, you may or may not achieve your goal of being one of the best, yet somewhere during the pursuit of that goal you will become a ballet dancer. The key is to choose.

Choosing which mountain to climb is one of the most important decisions you'll make because it determines what direction you'll take in your life. What does your mountain look like? You may be thinking of changing jobs or starting your own business. Perhaps you're struggling with an illness or facing problems in a relationship. Maybe you long to rediscover the hidden athlete inside yourself. In quiet moments you may hear the beckoning whispers from a lost dream or hidden talent. Please remember Frank Felt and take the time to look for the right mountain. It can change your life.

To "Choose Your Mountain" means that after you have looked at and reviewed all of the possibilities, you are the one to decide what mountain *you* want to climb. Just as important, you need to understand *why* you want to climb this mountain and then *how* you define success.

30. Intangible Energy

There is an incredible amount of intangible but powerful energy that you tap into when you are climbing the right mountain. It creates a positive force in your life that will help keep other kinds of negativity at bay. I'm sure you've experienced it. You get so wrapped up and involved in a project that your passion around it almost creates a shield that wards of negativity.

31. Four Ways to Find Your Mountain

There are basically four ways we find mountains: we choose freely, someone chooses for us, we find one by default, or life hands us a mountain. With free choice you may decide to do what Frank Felt did — quit your job and join the circus. Of course, until Frank truly chose his own mountain, he was climbing someone else's. If someone else is choosing your mountain for you, then you might find yourself in a position like the accountant who is so good at handling difficult clients that management decides to transfer her into sales.

Consider this scenario: There's an opening in the regional office in San Francisco, where you've always wanted to live, and you decide to go for it. It's the position you've wanted for a long time. You know you'd be perfect for it. You have the experience and the qualifications. In fact, your boss told you the job was yours if you wanted it. It's just that you never got around to sending in that resume. Now, you've been transferred and climbing a mountain in Timbuktu. You might say you didn't choose that mountain, yet perhaps you choose it by default.

And then there will be that time when life hands you a mountain. We'll all get one like this some day. The phone will ring and it will be that call you hoped you'd never get and you have a new mountain to climb.

It Doesn't Matter How You Find Your Mountain

People have different ways of finding their mountains, some just know and others need to explore before they find the right one and some end up with the right mountain out of default. What matters the most is if you find the right mountain, not how you find it.

Nancy, Cami and Retta are all climbing the same mountain; they are all attorneys at Jackson Walker. Yet they found their mountain in very different ways. Nancy Hamilton, as we discussed earlier, walked away from her mountain, yet found it being handed back to her by life.

Cami Boyd was a woman that just knew her mountain. She was nine years old and sitting with her father in a Chinese restaurant, the Forbidden City, when over lunch he asked her what she thought she might do when she grew up. Even though she was only in the fourth grade she was certain, she wanted to be an attorney. Cami remembers how surprised he was at her answer given that there were no other attorneys in the family. She has never wavered from her goal. Cami graduated from Syracuse University and is now a nationally respected commercial litigator and a partner in the Jackson Walker law firm out of Dallas, Texas with an expertise in intellectual property, trademark and copyright law.

Retta Miller is also a top trial attorney and partner with the Jackson Walker law firm. She specializes in litigation and arbitration involving securities, intellectual property, and business disputes. Often recognized for her significant community involvement, her most recent honor was to be the recipient of the 2003 Athena Award. You might think that to achieve this level of success that Retta must have always known that her mountain would be law, yet law wasn't her first career.

Retta started out her professional life with a degree in Home Economics from Oklahoma State University in 1975. It was only after several years in that field that she realized the career she had chosen wasn't right for her. In her own words she'd say, "It just didn't float my boat." Still undecided about what other career she wanted to pursue she took some aptitude tests and discovered she might make an excellent attorney. Even though she took the entrance exams and applied to law school at the last possible moment everything fell into place. Within twelve weeks, she found herself accepted into Northwestern University Law School. Retta found the right mountain, one that tapped into her passion and the rest is history. While at Northwestern, she received a number of job offers and she finally decided to accept a position with the Jackson Walker law firm in Dallas Texas. A decision she has never regretted.

32. Look at the Possibilities

It's time to claim your own mountain, big or small. All that really counts is that it's a mountain you believe in. Now, at this point there are usually three reactions I get from people. Some people know exactly what their mountain is. Some have so many mountains that it's difficult to narrow it down to just one. And still some others aren't sure what their mountain is.

If you already know your mountain, then as you read on I want you to challenge yourself to make sure this is the right mountain for you. If you're someone who has too many mountains—and most women do—then you really need to focus in on just one of them; and as you read on, the information may help you narrow down your choices. If you're someone who isn't sure you have one, then going through the following exercise may help you find yours.

33. Possibility Lists

Make a list of all the things that are of interest to you. Then explore them to see what sparks your passion. In fact, grab a friend or maybe a different friend every month and go to some new event/show/play/activity until you find something that grabs you. Areas to consider for "possibility lists" include:

- Interests, passions, and hobbies
- Personal strengths and weaknesses
- Organizations that you find interesting
- Things that are dear to you
- Experiences when you lost complete track of time
- Things you love to do that don't cost much

- Things you used to love doing but don't have time for anymore
- What did you want to be when you grew up?
- Services you would enjoy doing for others
- Your favorite daydreams

If you run short on ideas, visit your local bookstore, library, or telephone yellow pages. If you intend to make a list and then choose from it, make sure that you make some *great lists*, because the idea you choose can never be better than the ideas on that list. An Invisible Risk would be to limit the possibilities you consider. Don't allow yourself knowingly or unknowingly to start listening, believing, and living within the limitations others have placed on you. Consider all the possibilities, especially the outrageous ones.

34. Mind Map

If you aren't a list person, you might want to try mind mapping your ideas. Start with a central theme and branch out from there. You can have subgroups of subgroups of subgroups. The only limits are the ones you impose.

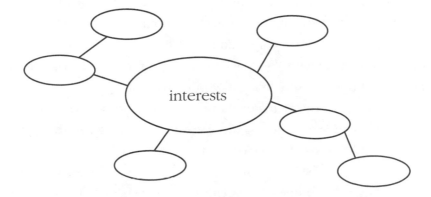

35. Mt. Everest Is Not the Tallest Mountain

Every personal mountain impacts us professionally, and every professional mountain impacts us personally. Sometimes people are hesitant to choose a mountain because they want the "perfect" mountain or because they feel as if theirs isn't important or large enough.

There is a general misconception that the right mountain can only be found by free choice. That's not always true. It doesn't matter how you find your mountain. Sometimes it doesn't even matter if you like the mountain. That was certainly the case with my best friend, Valari. She has been diagnosed with cancer five times over the course of the past several years. This was a series of mountains that life handed her. Valari's only choice was how she would climb them.

She claimed those mountains and chose to climb them with strength, courage, and determination. She did not back down from the challenge or hand this burden to anyone else, not for even a second. She got involved, did her research, called all the shots, picked the route, climbed each pitch, and took the risks one at a time. Not only did she not back down, Val did her fair share of handing out mountains to others, particularly her doctors. Rumor had it they snapped to attention when she entered a room — not out of fear, but out of their sheer respect and admiration for her. Valari had to focus on just one mountain to get the results she wanted, and today she's enjoying the rewards by living a wonderfully full life.

In reality it doesn't matter how you come across your mountain. Choosing it may not be any better in the long run than one you stumble across by accident. The best mountains are those you discover a passion around, no matter how it comes to you.

Interestingly, it does not seem to be the size of the goal that matters as much as its clarity and its significance to you. So, it is very important to not feel your mountain isn't valuable because it isn't huge. Trust that, if not already, there will be chapters in your life that will feel like you're climbing Mt. Everest. And there will be other chapters that in comparison seem much easier. Together these chapters make up a full life.

36. Looking for a Mountain?

If you're still unsure of your mountain, it could be for a variety of reasons. You may have just finished a climb and are looking, not quite ready for the next mountain. Perhaps you realize that you have been climbing someone else's mountain for so long that you are now searching for your own. Or maybe you aren't satisfied with the mountains you're climbing and are looking for a mountain that would be more meaningful.

Without any mountain in your life, it is easy to drift away from the person you want to be. So, if for some reason you feel you just aren't sure of a mountain I'd like you to consider making "finding your mountain" your mountain. It will prove to be an enlightening and interesting journey.

37. What Is Your Mountain?

What goal/challenge/dream is out there for you? To ensure it's the right mountain, ask yourself the following questions.

Do You Understand Your Mountain?

To be sure it is all you hope it will be, it's important to take the time to really get to know your mountain. Once you've zeroed in on what and why, it's time to learn as much as possible about your mountain. Turn to books, articles, the web, and others actually involved so that you go beyond a superficial look and learn about the realities of your goal.

Sometimes people pick a mountain that sounds attractive, but once they start the climb they realize it's not anything close to what they had expected. Can you remember the day when you couldn't wait to have the job you have right now? The one that drives you nuts! Remember waiting for the phone to ring hoping that you'd be offered this job? Remember thinking how everything would fall into place if only you could get this job? Remember how nice your supervisors were to you when they interviewed you? Perhaps they even took you out to lunch, and you haven't had time for lunch since you took this job.

It's important to understand your mountain, especially if it's of the Mt. Everest variety. If it is, you may want to even consider an internship. Try the mountain on for size before you buy. You certainly don't want to spend the time and money to become a veterinarian just to find out after you open your own practice that you don't like animals. You laugh, but this happens all the time.

Internship

The Garden of the Gods Club is an exclusive private property originally developed by H. L. Hunt's daughter, Margaret, and her husband, Al Hill, as a summer retreat for family and friends. Several years ago the club's administrators decided to bring in Destination Hotels & Resorts, a leading professional property management company, to further develop opportunities for the club. The original general manager who took on this project was so successful that he was promoted and moved to another property.

The club, now owned by Hunt Petroleum, was looking for the "perfect" general manager to handle their premier property. As the search went on, Leslie Carlson, Vice President of Operations for DH&R, stepped in to handle the transition. Although several candidates were presented, none of them quite fit the bill. In the meantime Leslie was immersed in the details of this complex property and intimately learning the business. At the same time, the Hunt family members still involved with the club were getting comfortable with Leslie running the show. In fact, they were so impressed with her that they asked if she was interested in taking over as the general manager.

As much as she loved working with the club, Leslie declined. She really enjoyed working with a variety of properties, she didn't want to give up her strategic corporate role, and she wasn't sure Hunt Petroleum was willing to give her the autonomy she would need to develop the property. However, she stayed on at the club as the search for the general manager continued. Four months later, Hunt Petroleum came to her and basically said, "Tell us what it would take to make you stay." By now Leslie had been on a long enough "internship" that she knew this was a career change she wanted to make. That is, *if* she could retain her strategic corporate role and *if* she was given the power and authority to make the necessary changes to grow the business. Everyone said, "Yes!" Leslie retained her corporate vice presidency and became the new general manager at the Garden of the Gods Club.

It was only through Leslie's "internship" that she was able to gather the information and the inspiration she needed to make this significant change in her life. Months later, she is confident that she took the right risk in the smartest way possible. It would have been a mistake to accept the position the first time. By waiting, she was able to take this job on her own terms, which in the end was the best for everyone involved.

Why This Mountain?

One way to understand whether or not this really is your mountain is to figure out how much passion you have for it. What are your own personal reasons for climbing this mountain? What is it about this mountain that fires you up? What is the attraction? What is it about this one that gives you motivation?

Does It Create a Compelling Future for You?

Do you find yourself thinking about your goal 24/7? Do you dream about it? Are you constantly talking to others about it? If you accomplish it, will it draw you closer to being the kind of person you'd like to be?

Is It a Worthy Goal?

Is this mountain worthy of your effort, time, and resources? Will climbing this mountain create something good for you or others? By the way, I certainly consider climbing for the pure fun, enjoyment, and exhilaration a worthy goal.

38. Whose Mountain Is It?

It was Chris's first day in kindergarten. Mrs. Smith announced, "Today we are going to draw a picture." Chris started drawing right away. Then Mrs. Smith said, "Stop, we aren't ready to begin yet." Chris thought, what do you mean? I'm ready.

Mrs. Smith then said, "Today we are going to draw a flower." Chris right away started drawing a black dragon flower that breathed fire. Mrs. Smith was walking along all the desks and looked at Chris's drawing. She said, "Don't you know how to draw a flower? I'll show you." She drew a red flower with a green stem.

Chris looked at Mrs. Smith's flower. It was an OK flower, but he liked his flower better. He looked around the room, and everyone else was drawing flowers just like Mrs. Smith's. He didn't want to get into any trouble on the first day of kindergarten, so he turned his page over and started drawing a red flower just like Mrs. Smith's. When Mrs. Smith came back by again she stopped, smiled, and told Chris, "You are a wonderful artist. Your flower looks just like mine."

You might be thinking that the mountain you have is really not your mountain—it is someone else's—but you still want to climb it. Maybe the mountain belongs to your boss, your husband, your children, or your best friend. If you find you want to climb someone else's mountain, then perhaps you are actually climbing a different mountain all together. Maybe the real mountain is having a relationship, keeping your job or getting a promotion. It may not be that you are climbing someone else's mountain. It may actually be just a route you're taking to achieve your own goal.

Do You Believe in Your Mountain?
Mattel

If you or your organization don't believe in the mountain then it will be very difficult to climb it successfully. I was asked to help start-up a new division of Mattel Toys called Emotions. Our goal was to develop and sell toy like products into gift channels of distribution. We weren't meeting with a lot of success, so we had this brainstorm. What if our parent company, Mattel Toys, gave us the rights to make a porcelain Barbie® doll?

It's important to understand that at Mattel, Barbie® is untouchable. Everyone knows that you just don't mess with Barbie.® We asked for permission anyway, and to our astonishment were told, "Fine. However, you're on your own." We should have known something was up, yet you know what they say, "Never look a gift horse in the mouth."

Our team didn't know the first thing about how to make a porcelain doll. I remember getting into my car and driving around to fabric shops in Beverly Hills looking for the perfect material. It turned out there weren't many fabric shops in Beverly Hills. Next, I was on airplanes traveling all over the world, trying to set up vendor networks. We found a gifted Russian sculptor, Igor Kunnonav, to make the original sculpture. I took the bullet train into the middle of Japan to work with older Japanese gentlemen who were among the best at porcelain casting and hand painting.

Some months later, our prototype porcelain Barbie® was done. We took her to Mattel for approval and they were shocked. It turned out that, without our knowledge, Mattel had tried for years to make a Barbie® out of porcelain. However, the company had determined that with all her delicate fingers and toes, she was impossible to replicate out of porcelain.

So why was it that Mattel Toys, with vast worldwide resources, couldn't make a porcelain Barbie® when a small untrained team at a small subsidiary could? Mattel simply didn't believe in the mountain. They were already successful, whereas we went after the development of a porcelain Barbie® as if the world depended on it.

This is proof positive of the old adage, "It's not the dog in the fight, it's the fight in the dog."

39. Defining Success

Summit Fever

Now it's time to determine how you define success. The single greatest loss of life on Mt. Everest in history occurred in 1996 because so many climbers defined success as getting to the summit at all costs. This is called *summit fever*, and with that definition of success people can make some bad choices.

When Sir Edmund Hillary was asked how he would feel if it were proven that George Mallory had actually reached the summit of Mt. Everest first, Hillary replied, "I personally have found it equally important to get back down the mountain alive." It's important to be on guard against summit fever with your own mountain and to avoid the temptation to reach your goal at any cost to either yourself or others.

Now it's time to define success for your mountain. It's critical that you understand the balance required for you to be happy or you may end up with a hollow victory. Most of us, if we were willing to set aside everything else in our lives and focus every ounce of our strength, energy, and thought into achieving a single goal would probably achieve success.

However, would giving up everything be worth it? What if there was no one there to share it with? What if it meant losing health or emotional stability? The Centers for Disease Control and Prevention recently released statistics that indicate that 80 percent of every health care dollar spent in this country is related to stress. Sometimes I think we spend our youth for wealth and then our wealth for health.

How would you define success if you were running a marathon? What if you won the race but pushed yourself so hard you were never able to run again? What if you didn't win the race but you finished it when others thought you didn't have it in you? What if you ran the race and didn't finish because of a twisted ankle, yet you became best friends with the medic who helped you? Who won?

Success Components

To find meaningful success requires that you define success based on your own personal needs. Even though this can be a difficult task, defining success clearly by your own standards will make it easier to achieve. The categories listed below are a good place to start, but it's important to customize this list to fit you, so please add any and all other categories or subcategories that you think would be of benefit.

It's critical that you're clear on how you define success because the route you plan in the next section will be based on your definition of success. If you define success by simply summiting Mt. Everest, then you won't need to pack those extra oxygen tanks for getting back down.

I've found that there are essentially six components that cover most of the bases. Consider how you might define success for your mountain as it relates to these categories (feel free to add more categories):

    Professionally
    Personally

Financially
Emotionally
Physically
Spiritually

*"How many cares one loses when one
decides not to be something but to be someone."*
—*Coco Channel*

How do you define success for your mountain? What prescription would you write for yourself? Perhaps thinking of it as a recipe will help. Most recipes share some common ingredients like, flour, sugar and eggs. Yet each recipe is unique and creates its own end result. You may need 4 cups of one ingredient, a teaspoon of another and just a dash of spice to give it pizzazz. As you grow and change over time so will your taste and the recipe will need to be adjusted. Following are some lists of sample questions to help you start thinking about what your own personal recipe might look like.

40. Professionally

What type of job?
What type of organization?
What hours?
What days of the week do your work?
How are you paid, salary, commission, or bonus?
How are you evaluated?

How challenging do you want the work to be?

Do you work on a team or alone?

Who do you work for?

What kind of title do you want?

Are there additional perks?

41. Personally

How much free time do you have?

Where do you want to live?

How close do you want to be to family and friends?

Do you have a good support group?

Do you have access to the activities you love?

Are you involved in healthy relationships?

Do you have children?

Is there time for you?

Do you spend quality time with those you're close to?

42. Financially

How much money do you need to make?

What kind of house do you need?

How many cars do you want?

Do you have enough money beyond the house payment to enjoy life?

Do you have enough in your savings in case something happens?

Is your retirement set?

Is money how you measure success?

43. Emotionally

How often do you laugh?

How much stress can you handle?

How do you relax?

Do you ever relax?

Do you have time to play?

How do you play?

Do you feel satisfied at the end of the day?

How well do you get along with others?

Do you feel emotionally resilient?

Do you take time out for yourself?

44. Physically

Are you healthy?

Are you fit/strong?

Do you work out consistently?

Are you eating well?

Do you get the sleep you need?

Do you feel rested?

Do you have a great network of doctors?

45. Spiritually

Are you at peace with your soul?

Are you finding ways to help others?

46. How Do You Define Success?

Above is only a sampling of possible ingredients. Make a note if you think it will help of how you might define success as it relates to your mountain.

47. Challenging Your Definition of Success

Renata Fusca

Success can be defined in many different ways. The Odyssey of the Mind is a program designed to encourage creative problem solving and risk taking in children. The project during one year was to create a device that would move across water. All the teams except one came up with some great yet traditional approaches to solve the problem. The other team's idea was way out there. They decided to try to duplicate the way the Renata Fusca, a water spider, moved across a lake. They designed a device that would recreate the same type of tension on the water surface as this spider.

Their device failed. In fact, it sank during the competition; however, the judges agreed it was by far the most ingenious idea they had ever seen at the contest. Even though the idea failed, they needed to reward that team's creativity. They were also wise enough to realize that if the only thing they rewarded was success, they would be teaching the children to submit only ideas that would work rather than pursuing their best ideas. It would all but seal the fate that every team would start thinking in terms of *not failing* rather than *winning*.

The judges in their wisdom challenged their definition of success and decided to broaden it. They created a whole new award, the Renata Fusca. It holds a very esteemed and special place in the competition. Interestingly, it is one of the few awards not given yearly. Instead, it is saved for that person or team who exhibits exceptional creativity and innovation.

Rewarding Risks that Don't Turn Out

If your definition of success is founded in only one category then you may want to reconsider. As far as risk goes every parent, every individual, and every organization wants others to take risks as long as they can guarantee they'll work. However, this type of attitude is stifling and sends one message: It's okay to take chances that are safe. This really defeats the entire premise of risk taking because there is no option for an outcome that is unexpected. Yet, it is our failures that create unexpected outcomes which in turn provide us, individually and collectively, with the giant leaps in performance and development.

If you want to make a change in your own risk taking ability or in that of those on your team, then you might want to consider reward risks that didn't work as long as they were on target strategically and tackled in a smart way. I'm not suggesting that you reward wild shots or dumb chances. A smart risk is one that has go/no go criteria built in so that losses can be contained. However, if you begin rewarding risks that don't turn out as planned yet have all the elements of a Renata Fusca, you'll start sending a new message: It's okay to take smart, strategic risks.

Definitions Are Dynamic

Now that you have defined success for yourself, take a moment to challenge and reconsider. Is there anything you might want to change? Even if there is nothing that you want to change today please be aware that how you define success should not be written in stone. What works today may not work tomorrow. Your definition will continue to evolve and change as you evolve and grow. At twenty you may have been active enough that you didn't need to carve out time to workout. However, after fifty, finding time to exercise may become far more critical.

48. The Power that Comes from Choosing the Right Mountain

Choose a mountain and you'll find the talents to climb it.

If I asked you not to think about a yellow spotted purple dragon, what would you be thinking about? We tend to get what we focus on. Imagine that you were just told you are going to compete in the next Olympics to take place twelve months from today. You must compete; however, you can choose which event. In fact you have a guaranteed spot on the team. Which event would you choose? How would your focus change? How would you train? What else in your life would change? Imagine, this same effect created with any mountain.

Choose a mountain and the future starts organizing it.

Setting the path creates a magnetic power that helps draw it toward you and you toward your goal. You'll start finding the information, people, and energy you'll need to climb. Once you are clear on your goal and committed to it, you'll be amazed at how events start shaping themselves.

Remember the last time the thought of buying a car went through your mind? If you're like most of us, your first thought was, "No, I don't really need a new car, the one I have is fine."

Then you made some kind of decision. You dismissed the idea and went in a different direction. Or, you started down the path of justifying how you really did need a new car. If you went down this path, all of a sudden you began to notice all the car ads on television and in the newspapers and magazines. Yesterday, you hadn't even seen them, yet today they're everywhere. You find yourself talking to friends about their cars. You stop by a dealership just to look. You find a car that is really cool. There just aren't many out there like it. Then they offer you this incredible deal that you just can't pass up. You own a new car. You drive it off the showroom floor, and then everywhere you look, there are cars just like it. Hmmm...

There's a big difference between making a commitment and having a strong interest.

Now that you have narrowed down your list, you should be clear on whose mountain it is, why you're climbing it, and what your mountain involves. Now it's time to commit. Whether you have chosen to start walking every day, lose ten pounds, or change jobs, not much will happen with only a casual interest.

I did a program for Lincoln/Mercury, and the top executive there decided to share his mountain and his route with his entire team. This gentleman was a very successful businessman. He was quite comfortable with both professional and physical risk taking. His mountain was one he had wanted to climb for years yet found more and more difficult to tackle. His mountain was telling his parents he loved them. His route was to do this during his family reunion coming up in three weeks.

Why do you think he was willing to share such a personal mountain with his team? One thing was certain: He gained a tremendous amount of respect from his team for having the courage to share his goal with them. Yet, I don't believe that this man was having a "soft" moment. I think he was a very smart man who knew that by sharing his mountain he was virtually guaranteeing his own success. There wasn't any way he would want to come back from his vacation and have to tell one hundred other people that he had backed down. He wrote me a letter the week he returned; very proud that he had indeed reached his summit.

There is power in declaring your mountain to others. Once you've committed to yourself, start telling others of your goal to help ensure your own success. It's odd how we are often more willing to break a deal with ourselves than we're willing to go back on a goal that we've shared with others.

"I know for sure that what we dwell on is who we become."
—Oprah Winfrey

49. Invisible Risk Journal

Insights	Actions

Insights	*Actions*

Insights	Actions

Plan Your Route

"It is not how much we do, but how much love we put in the doing. It is not how much we give, but how much love we put in the giving."
— *Mother Teresa of Calcutta*

50. Potential Routes

Blending Qualitative and Quantitative Information

For every mountain there are hundreds, if not thousands, of possible routes. Every mountain requires a different plan of attack based on who's climbing and how they define success. The key is to create a route that will fit your own interests, abilities, and needs. This requires both objective and subjective information.

As an example, traditional project management may determine that the best plan for going back to school (for a person who is working full time and on a tight budget) would be for that person to continue working and pick up one or two classes every semester until they finish their degree. For some this might be the perfect solution. This route would appeal to them because it fits their personality. For many others that plan would limit their chances for success. Based on their personalities the right route would be quite different. They would be better off quitting their jobs, getting a student loan, and taking extra credits to finish school as quickly as possible. This route may work better because they would see it as a way to keep up their passion, get a better job sooner, pay off the loan faster, and move on to the next mountain. The best route is the one that matches how you define success while it blends qualitative and quantitative information.

51. Serious Mountains Require Serious Planning

In today's world of "too much to do and too little time," most of us do not actually sit down and create a detailed plan of attack for our mountains. In many cases just thinking through the plan can be enough. However, if you are tackling a mountain that could seriously jeopardize your life, finances, career, emotional health, or spiritual well-being, then it's critical you take the time and acquire the expertise to create a full-scale plan. If you don't, then you won't be taking an Intelligent Risk.

To do this I suggest you pick up a project management book that deals with your specific goal and potentially find an expert in this area who can help you. If you're considering anything that could seriously impact your life but you don't plan, you are simply taking a dumb chance.

52. IntelligentRisking Foundation

I'm a big believer in doing everything possible to synthesize the complex into something that is straightforward, easy to understand, and memorable. Therefore, the IntelligentRisking Foundation consists of just six key questions to remember:

Who?

What?

When?

Where?

Why?

How?

Using the IntelligentRisking Foundation you'll be able to look at quantitative information, found in traditional project management, as well as qualitative information, found in your own self-awareness. Only when you're able to blend these different factors and types of information can you begin to craft a route that will work for you.

As you seek quantitative or tangible information you'll need to look at the issues that you can actually measure. You'll look at what you need versus what you have and identify how you intend to bridge the gap.

As you look for qualitative information you'll want to look at the subjective side and the intangibles involved with your mountain. You'll want to explore your own perceived strengths, weaknesses, and preferences taking into account any factors that are significant enough to effect your decisions.

The first step is to determine what you need. This requires information and doing your homework to find out as much as possible about your mountain. In climbing this is called getting "Beta." This involves research that includes reading, studying, and spending time exploring your mountain. It also means talking to others who have climbed similar mountains and learning from their successes and failures.

As women we need to remind ourselves that by definition a risk is a risk. We'll never have everything we need. It will never be perfect. We will make mistakes and need to adjust. We should focus on our strengths and plan a route that will capitalize on them. If you know you are not good at accounting, then hire someone who is; don't spend your own time and energy in that area.

Below is a list of specific questions tied to each of the six IntelligentRisking Foundation questions intended to get you started. As you read through the questions, those that most directly apply to you and your risk will probably stand out. The ones on this list may trigger other questions you need to ask. Please feel free to write down your answers, other questions as you think of and notes to help you develop the best route.

53. Who?

Who are the right people for your team?
Who is on your team that shouldn't be?
Who isn't on your team that should be?
Who else is passionate about your mountain?
Who believes in you and wishes you success?
Who doesn't believe in you and secretly hopes you fail?
Who are you trying to impress?
Who can help you?
Who could hurt or sabotage you?
Who will benefit?
Who else is involved?
Who else has control over the outcome?
Who is pressuring you?
Who is holding you back?
Who are you trying to please?

54. What?

What are the risks?
What are the rewards?
What is your passion?
What is the worst that could happen?
What is the best that could happen?
What is the most realistic outcome?
What can you afford to lose?
What can you do to reduce the risks?
What can you do to increase the rewards?
What information do you need?

What equipment, supplies, skills, training, talents,
and other resources will you need?

What equipment, supplies, skills, training, talents,
and other resources do you have?

What is the gap?

What can you do to lessen the gap?

What can you do to improve your chances for success?

What makes this risk necessary?

What needs to happen?

What tasks are involved?

What do you need to do?

What do others need to do?

What milestones do you need to achieve?

What go/no go decision points are necessary?

What do you need to control?

What do you need to let go of?

What filters are you using?

What are your strengths?

What are your preferences?

What are your weaknesses?

55. When?

When will you start?

When will you have what you need?

When do you want/need to reach your milestones?

When do you want/need to accomplish your
tasks/objectives/goals?

When do you need your equipment and supplies?

When should you make your first move?

When would be the best time to act?

When would be the worst time to act?

When will you need to reevaluate?

When should you set your go/no go points?

When will you need to capitalize on your strengths?

When should you be wary of your weaknesses?

When is your olympic moment of opportunity?

56. Where?

Where will you find the expertise you'll need?

Where will you find the people you need on your team?

Where will you get the supplies you need?

Where will you get the equipment you need?

Where will you establish your base camp?

Where will you get the training you need?

Where will you get the resources you need?

Where will you get the funding you need?

Where will this take place?

Where will you turn for help?

Where will you keep everything?

Where will you turn for support?

Where will you get the information and research you need?

Where will you need your go/no go decision points?

57. Why?

Why this mountain?
Why this team?
Why this risk?
Why now?
Why this route?
Why are you passionate about this?
Why are you afraid?
Why are you waiting?
Why not?

58. How?

How big is the gap between what you
    have and what you need?
How will you close the gap and reduce your risk?
How will you improve your chances for success?
How will you find the team/support you need?
How will you get the equipment, supplies, skills,
    training, talents, and other resources you'll need?
How will you manage your strengths/weaknesses
    and preferences?
How will you know when it's time to reevaluate?
How will you challenge your filters?
How will you get what you need?
How will you train/prepare?
How will you hold onto your passion?
How will you tame your fears?
How much stuff do you need?

How much time will it all take?

How much will this cost?

How much can you afford?

59. What's Your Route?

How, What, When, Where, Why, and How?

It's now time for you to determine the best route for you to climb your mountain. As you think it through, remember that it's important that your route capitalize on your strengths while managing your weaknesses and that your route is defined to help you reach success as you've previously defined it. A route that works beautifully for one person can spell disaster for the next. Your route should be uniquely yours.

You may find it helpful to jot down in the journal some of the basics of your plan—who, what, when, where, why, and how.

60. Do Not Marry Your Plan

Route Finding Is a Dynamic Process

No matter how much you study, how many people you interview, and how much time you've spent planning, once you're up on the rock your perspective changes. Nothing is ever quite the way you anticipated. Route finding is a fluid, dynamic process that changes based on numerous variables including weather, team endurance, supplies, etc. You'll find the same true on your mountain. Once you start your climb, things will change and you'll need to be flexible on the route, trusting in your own resourcefulness to get around the obstacles you'll encounter.

It's important to think through your plan, to stay flexible and then begin testing it. This is the truest way to see if your plan will fit you, your style, and your needs. It's critically important to avoid becoming so vested in your plan that you refuse to deviate from it. Flexibility to adopt and adapt your plan to the real world will best determine your chances for success.

The Right Route Is Critical to Success

All of us know someone who is brilliant yet struggles to find success. I'm convinced that unless they've chosen the wrong mountain, it comes down to having chosen the wrong route.

Have you noticed how interviewing for a new job is a lot like a first date? Everyone is at his or her best, extremely polite and optimistic. I'm convinced the best day on any job is the day before you start, because on that fateful first day of work you begin to understand that things aren't quite as wonderful as you thought.

That's how it was for me when I started working for Coors. Since I was going to be responsible for new product development and sales on my first day, I wanted to find out exactly how many "new" products were truly ready to be go. The response was, "None." And I thought, "Well, that makes it harder." Then I asked, "What where you talking about during my interview?" That's when they started to explain.

As it turns out, Joe Coors had gone on an overnight business trip and had only taken one dress shirt. That's what men tend to do, pack one shirt for one meeting. Ladies, if we went on an overnight business trip we'd pack options. Anyway, when he went to put on his one shirt it had three broken buttons. He was furious and decided right there that Coors would make an unbreakable men's dress shirt button. He had the passion, and the mountain was clear. Even the route was fairly obvious since Coors not only made beer but was also a huge manufacturer of technical ceramics.

Joe Coors decided that this button would make the perfect product to start up a company, Ceramicon, to launch ceramic products into the consumer arena. The company spent the next two years working on the development of an unbreakable button. They were successful with a virtually indestructible button made out of Transformation Toughened Zirconium. This button was so tough it could practically stop a bullet.

They were planning on success and had lined up Arrow, one of the largest dress shirt manufacturers in the world, to buy the button. It appeared to be a match made in heaven. One slight catch! The button cost more for Coors to make than Arrow would ever dream of paying for it. The obvious solution; find a way to lower the price. They tried everything imaginable, and no matter how much they reduced the cost, it was still too expensive. Finally they gave up on the button determining that it just couldn't be sold.

When I came into the company I was fresh, I wasn't burned out on the button. But when you sign on for any new business/new product/sales type job the first thing you are given is your dollar goal, and it doesn't matter if you don't have a product to sell. So when I started asking about what products were ready and they said, "None" I knew I needed to get creative. I asked them to tell me more about this button.

It's important to understand that the technical ceramic industry has an industrial mindset, where the margins are low and volumes high. They may only sell a product for a few pennies but they sell millions and millions of them so the math still works. My background on the other hand is quite different. If you've ever been to Disney World or bought a Hallmark Card you know how expensive both are, so you might say I came from a premium pricing background where I learned how to position, market, and sell the intangibles.

With nothing to lose and a sales goal to make, I decided to go after the button. I knew we needed a different route to get up this mountain so I drew on my own background of marketing premium products. The button was given a name, The Diamond Z. It was given its own logo. We doubled the price. It was now not just an unbreakable button, it was now an environmentally friendly alternative to all pearl and shell buttons. Our first sales calls were not to mass marketers like Arrow, they were to top name designers such as Ralph Lauren. The first order came from the environmentally conscientious Nordstroms. That button, the one that "couldn't be sold", became one of the single most profitable products in the company.

Coors had the passion, they knew the mountain but they had chosen the wrong route and then were unwilling to adjust to the obstacles they encountered. Although this book is not specifically about diversity this is a perfect example of why diversity is so valuable. When you create a team that blends diverse backgrounds you gain additional perspectives, expertise and abilities from which to better tackle difficult challenges.

Just as with Coors you can be clear about your mountain and have a tremendous amount of passion; however, if you choose the wrong route you will struggle to find success. The key is to plan a route that plays to your strengths and then if it isn't working don't just quit look for alternative routes by remaining flexible, relying on your resourcefulness and trusting your instincts.

Trust Your Intuition

Have you ever believed in an idea that everyone else thought was crazy? J. Madden, a successful real estate developer in the Denver area, thought it would be a great idea to build an upscale athletic club in the Denver Tech Center. He wanted this to be a smart risk. He hired a consultant to research and evaluate the viability of his concept. The facts were gathered. The consultant's information led them to conclude... it was not a good idea.

This information just didn't seem to match J.'s intuition. His "gut" told him it would work. To go ahead with his idea in the face of this research would be a significant risk. J. struggled with trying to balance the analysis with what he believed in his heart. His decision? He modified his plans, changed his route slightly, and then made his crux move by building the Greenwood Athletic Club. Ten years later, it is one of the most successful health clubs in the country. He proved that success means blending information with inspiration — listening to your intuition and then taking dynamic action.

61. What Is Your Backup Plan?

Contingency Plans

Perhaps it's because of my background that I love contingency plans. They have saved me so many times that they are second nature to me now. Even if I'm just setting up a coffee date with someone I'm giving them my cell phone number or picking out an alternative place to meet, just in case.

Now that you've created a route, it's good to keep in mind what contingency plans might be useful. If you know who you want on the team and they aren't available, how will you adjust? If you can't get the training, what will you do? What if the money runs out too soon? Planning for contingencies requires that you ask the "What if?" question for every aspect of your plan and develop a contingency.

You will need to ask the "What if?" from both a negative and a positive perspective. This is a lesson I learned over and over again during my new product and business development days. For example we needed to ask "What if?" in case a toy was a flop so that we would be prepared to minimize our losses. We also needed to ask "What if?" in case a toy was a huge hit, ironically for the same reason, to minimize our losses. Toy cycles or life spans are very short so we need to have contingency plans in place to both immediately stop production and immediately expand production based on the new product's success. If the toy took off and we couldn't meet demand we'd miss out on a tremendous sales opportunity which would translate into lost dollars.

As we discussed in the beginning of this chapter, the more serious the risk, the more planning and contingency planning is required.

62. Spontaneous Risk

Spontaneous vs. Planned Risk

There are several different kinds of risk. We've been looking at the type of risk that is premeditated and thought through. Yet, often we face spontaneous risks where you simply have to jump in and trust that you'll figure out the route as you go along.

Sometimes You Just Have to Jump In

Sometimes you just find yourself in a situation that requires you to take a risk and there's no time to plan. That was the case for Barb Weiman as she was visiting a high school in an unofficial role, delivering brownies for her granddaughter's birthday. Even though Barb has dedicated herself to children as an educational counselor for almost fifty years, she hadn't anticipated what was about to happen.

It was an alternative high school where the students came from a number of different schools around the city. There were gang members from opposing gangs and the fighting between them had escalated to a red alert status. If the teachers heard a gang call, they locked the classroom doors and called the police.

The school was set up in a Y floor plan. Barb had just gotten to the middle of the three intersecting halls when she heard a cry from the end of one of the hallways. She'd had enough experience to know the meaning of that ominous sound. Then she heard a responding cry from an opposing gang at the end of the opposite hallway. Barb was caught in the middle. Even though Barb has a reputation for not being intimidated by anyone or anything, she still wasn't really prepared for two rival gangs bearing down on her ready to fight.

Not knowing exactly what to do, she trusted her instincts and held her ground. Seeing Grandma in the middle of the hall wasn't exactly what either gang expected, so they were momentarily caught off guard. Knowing she wouldn't have the upper hand for long, Barb started passing out brownies and ordering everyone to try them. Fortunately, Barb is a fabulous cook, and with just one bite she had these would-be combatants hooked and literally eating out of the palm of her hand. This was quite a shock to the police, who showed up minutes later anticipating a gang war. Barb turned around what could have been a very disastrous situation with her quick wits, willingness to risk, and some incredible brownies.

Sometimes You Get Pushed in

I have always envied those who always knew what they wanted to do when they grew up. I wasn't that lucky. The only thing I knew for sure growing up is that I wanted to do something that would make a difference. I wanted to help people. Even though starting your own business is a risk that most people would want to plan, it isn't how I went about it.

When I had my first child I decided that my mountain was to be a great mom so I left the corporate arena and went the more traditional route by staying home full time. Well, after having three boys in three years I was having serious doubts. I remember leaving Target with nine bags of disposable diapers and the young man ringing up my purchases asked me if I knew I had picked up three different sizes of diapers. I assured him that I was perfectly aware as all three of were in diapers at the same time. At that moment something clicked and I knew the "traditional route" wasn't right for me.

I decided that perhaps a consulting opportunity where I could work part-time might be the answer. The first two organizations I contacted both offered me full time jobs. Not what I was looking for, but I decided to try giving the working full time route a go. Many of my friends were climbing their mountains successfully with this route so why not me? I accepted a full-time position with Coors and hired a professional nanny to look after the boys.

It took almost three years to decide that this route wasn't right for me either. That's when I realized I needed to sit down and seriously think through how I defined success. I was still working full time but I had started toying around with some various options in my mind. I wondered if cutting back on the travel and perhaps working only four days a week in the office might make a good compromise. I decided to test the water and throw that option out to my boss. The following day we talked over lunch, and by the end of that day I was no longer an employee of Coors but a consultant, and Coors was my first customer.

I honestly didn't know what hit me. It certainly isn't how I'd recommend anyone start their own business. It turned out to be the right route for me, however, if I'd have known at the time how hard this would be, how much blood, sweat, and tears it would take, I'd never have tried. In the first year I lost $40,000. Do you know why I lost $40,000? Because it's all the money I had. If I'd have had $60,000, I'd have lost that too. At some point when your back is against the wall, if you want it badly enough, you'll find a way to make it work.

When you travel a lot, you tend to see a lot of movies on airplanes. Last summer I saw *Maid in Manhattan* seven times. The one line I loved in that movie came as the maid was fired and she found out the butler was also leaving. She tried to apologize to him. He turned to her and said something like, "Life has a funny way of opening doors that you should have found for yourself." The key is to recognize them and walk through while they are still open.

No doubt you're thinking, "What does all this mean to me?" It means that decisions involving risk can come flying at you before you've had your first cup of coffee, or they may come as the result of careful planning. Life is a wonderful mix of the spontaneous and the scheduled. The key is to live life to the fullest and trust that IntelligentRisking will help you with the pivotal decisions you'll face no matter what.

63. No Perfect Plan

Whether the risk is planned or spontaneous we are not looking for a perfect plan. We are looking for a great plan. The truth is that some of us love the planning part more than the doing part. We spend all of our time acquiring information. It's easy to use this planning process as an excuse not to start. It's easy to argue that we need a solid plan with every possibility thought out. People get so caught up in creating the perfect plan that they completely miss their window of opportunity. There is no perfect plan, so set yourself a time limit. Do the best you can and then start taking some kind of action to test your plan and create some momentum.

64. Plan Your Route Journal

Insights	Actions

Insights	*Actions*

Insights	*Actions*

Build Your Courage

*"You gain strength, courage, and confidence by every experience
in which you really stop to look fear in the face.
You must do the thing that you think you cannot do."*
—*Eleanor Roosevelt*

65. Courage Touchstone

I have an unusual perspective on courage. I think that coming up with courage is fairly easy. Think about it. You want to try something new. It feels exciting. You tell some friends. They get excited for you. The momentum builds. What is extraordinarily difficult is holding on to your courage when times get tough. When all your friends are gone and you're all by yourself wondering if you're doing the right thing, that's when it gets hard.

This struggle with courage is something that we can anticipate happening because it happens to even the bravest people. We can prepare by having a "courage touchstone." Even though we are the only ones who can give ourselves courage, we need a courage touchstone, a person, a place, a time, or a memory that will help us reconnect with our own courage.

Sasha

For myself I go back a few summers to when I met Alexander Supernov. I was meeting my friend Brian; however, when he showed up he was on his way to grant a rush wish for the Make-A-Wish Foundation. He'd been a wish grantor for many years and invited me to go with him. I'm a very spontaneous person, so I jumped in the car without thinking it all through. The wish was to a little Russian boy who, with his mother, was brought to Denver to receive treatment for his leukemia. His nickname was Sasha. Since neither Sasha nor his mother spoke any English, an interpreter was also at the house. Make-A-Wish, as with all organizations, requires a ton of paperwork. Brian, the interpreter, and Sasha's mother sat at the kitchen table filling out forms, which left me alone with Sasha.

Sasha was seven years old and at the time my sons were

five, eight, and nine, so you know he had a special place in my heart. When I left that day I realized two truths: (1) I had fallen hopelessly in love with Sasha, and (2) No matter the circumstances, no matter where they're from, when it's time to go, little boys can't find their shoes.

Sasha's wish to visit Disney World was granted. However, just coming to America was like Disney World to him, so this trip was the frosting on the cake. I hope that everyone has the opportunity to see a wish like this come true. The transformation in Sasha was dramatic. He came back with so much life and vitality it was like meeting a new child.

Now, I was faced with a difficult choice. I knew Sasha didn't really know anyone or have any friends in Denver. Should I invite him over and include him in my life? That would be a risk. I was already in love with him, so what if something did happen? It would break my heart and also probably affect my own boys. How would that impact them if something happened to someone their own age? Then I thought, but we have so much to offer him, we certainly had all the toys a seven-year-old boy could want. I decided to call a family meeting. I explained to my boys that Sasha had a life-threatening illness, and did they think we should invite him over to play? They looked at me as if I'd grown another head. Boy, play-of course we should invite him over. Why are we having a family meeting about something like this? They even had their heads shaved so he wouldn't feel out of place.

I was nervous about having Sasha over to our house since my boys are not quiet by any stretch of the imagination. I told them that Sasha didn't have the strength they had so I asked them to tone it down a bit. I started them all out playing cards. After a short while, they were all bored to tears. That's when my son Nick looked over at Sasha and said, as only an eight-year-old boy could, "You don't look like you are dying to me...let's go play." And they all took off!

You see, my sons were willing to give Sasha the gift that I wasn't. They treated him just like a regular kid. They ended up terrorizing the entire neighborhood. Over the summer we all fell in love with Sasha. I spent the summer pursuing various legal possibilities to keep Sasha here with us while he got better, but in August the doctors determined the treatment was no longer effective. Sasha and his mother would have to return to Russia. On the morning he left, as I was seeing him off he looked at me and said, "Please don't make me go. I want to stay here with you." I had to say goodbye. In October of that year, Sasha died. Did he break my heart? Yes! Was it worth the risk? Yes!

Some of the greatest lessons I have learned in my life I learned from that little Russian boy who spoke little English. He taught me to take the risk of living life. Few of the risks we take will turn out just the way we plan. Yet, if you take the right risk for the right reason it always turns out somehow.

Sasha taught me that more important than the outcome, it's who you become for having taken a risk you believe in. Because of Sasha I'm now on the bone marrow donor transplant list as well as a wish grantor for Make-A-Wish Foundation. I have a wish board up in my office, and every time life gets tough, I walk over to it and my problems fall back into perspective.

When ever I lose sight of my courage — and I do just like everyone else — I think of Sasha. He will always be my courage touchstone, and I will always hear his voice say, "I believe in you. You can do this."

Take a moment and think of where you will turn when your own fears overwhelm you. What person, place, time, or memory will help you reconnect with your own courage? By the way, I've been asked this question many times and the answer is, "No, chocolate does not count as a courage touchstone."

66. What Are Your Risks?

You have chosen your mountain and you have probably started thinking about what risks are associated with climbing it. Two friends can take on the same mountain and yet they will see the risks quite differently. One woman may feel that losing touch with those she's worked so closely with is a risk while the other woman may see losing touch as a reward.

Ask yourself, realistically, if you take on this goal what is the worst that can happen? Take the time to note down all the significant risks that come to mind.

67. Have You Faced Your Fears?

If you run from your fears, they will chase you.

Given the risks associated with your mountain, what are your fears? Why do you feel these fears? What in your past or in your personal makeup contributes to these fears? What fears do you need to face?

Identifying your fears requires that you look behind the risks to see what it is you're actually afraid of. It requires that you look a little deeper to understand what it is in your past or your personality that has contributed to your fear. Facing your fears is different from identifying and understanding them. It is much more difficult.

I've been paragliding for about five years now. However, I've never had the luxury of flying often. Last year I had a rough landing and broke my tailbone. It was clearly pilot error. Knowing that it was my own fault did not help my confidence. I still had the passion to fly, but I found myself making all kinds of excuses to ensure I didn't have time to fly. Finally, I got to the point where I had run out of good excuses, and I decided I'd get back in the saddle (or harness) again. I knew I was a little nervous, but I didn't realize how scared I was until we were actually driving up to launch. I started crying! No one was more surprised than I. Honestly, I had no idea I had so much fear that I hadn't dealt with.

My greatest fear was that I was inadequate, that I didn't have the skill, knowledge, or competency to fly. That is a scary thought, and it should be. The last thing anyone wants is a pilot up in the air that isn't qualified. Yet, I know that I have excellent ground handling skills, and launch and landing skills. That's the critical part because that's where you get hurt. I realized that day that understanding and talking about your fears is not the same as *facing* them.

Once I faced my fears and got past the tears, I still wasn't ready to fly. I could have, but I wasn't prepared emotionally. However, I was ready to get my paragliding wing out and practice. I clearly remember going up on the hill. I was the only woman there, which is not unusual. I spent the day practicing and watching the other pilots. The practice reduced my fear while watching the other pilots fly fueled my passion. I had made the shift. My passion was now greater than my fear and I was ready to launch. They say you only have one "first" flight and that no other flight will ever compare, but that flight certainly came close.

Take some time to think through and understand what fears you may have. I realize that this is a difficult challenge.

What is it that may stop you from reaching your goal? What fears may lure you into quitting too soon? It may help to write them down next to your risks.

68. What Are Your Rewards?

Now, what do you see as the rewards for taking the risk of climbing this mountain? What are the benefits you see? What will you gain? What is the best that can happen? Rewards are also subjective so please take the time to write out all the rewards that you think are possible.

69. What Are Your Passions?

What passion do these rewards tap into for you? What is it about these rewards that fire you up? What are your passions? Why this mountain? What will help you see it through the tough times? Please take the time to write down your passions so that this list will help you push past your fears.

70. Build Your Courage

Passion greater than fear equals courage. Do you have the courage you need to tackle your mountain? If not then you need to find ways to build your passion and reduce your fear.

I think that even though our mountains may be quite different, we all share basically the same fears. I'll take a chance and share with you my personal struggle over writing this book. The risk I saw was that I might not be able to clearly articulate my thoughts in a way that would help other women. I was afraid that I might say the wrong thing or too much or too little. I took my responsibility to write a great book so seriously that I wanted the book to be perfect. That risk tapped into my fear that I wouldn't be good enough. The reason I share such personal feelings is to ensure that you understand "everyone" has fears. The key is to face them and then do what you need to do even if it isn't perfect.

The reward I saw in writing this book was the possibilities of helping other women see within themselves the talent, wisdom, and potential that I saw in them. The other reward I saw was sending a strong message to my sons about not giving up when it gets hard. You see, I had told them I was going to write this book five years ago. Months ago Joey asked me what happened to my book. I didn't have a good answer. I knew that even though I might be willing to let myself down, I was not willing to let my sons see me give up on a dream. I did not want to be a quitter in their eyes. Both of these rewards tapped into my passion to make a difference. Even though my fears held me back, my passion finally won out. You are holding the proof in your hands.

71. Reducing Your Fear

Fear is a double-edged sword. On the one hand, it keeps you safe. On the other hand, it can stop you from doing so many things. Risk by definition is always risky so there will always be some fear. The key is not to eliminate your fears. The key is to feel the fear without letting it control you; to understand your fears and then make a choice that is your own. There are many ways to reduce your fears. Let's look at a couple. One is feeling prepared. The other is identifying, understanding, and facing your fears.

Preparation

Being prepared is following through on the plan you developed to acquire the training, resources, equipment, and supplies you need. The greater the gap between what you think it will take and what you believe you have the more fear you will feel.

Surround Yourself with Support

This is an old, tried and true formula that most of us know by heart. However, it is still a very powerful tactic. If you have support from family, friends, and coworkers then you are well on your way to success. If you interact on a consistent basis with others who share your passion, your path will be easier. If, however, you find yourself surrounded with doomsayers who constantly remind you of your weaknesses then you are facing an uphill fight.

This is where being proactive is critical. Knowing that those who are negative are going to hold you back, you need to make a choice about whether you will accept, change, or reject those who are negative. It's up to you.

72. Increasing Your Passion

Again, there are many ways to increase your passion. We'll look at several. One is to visualize yourself successfully reaching your goal. Another is to surround yourself with people who believe in you and support your mountain.

73. Women Supporting Women

Jackson Walker

When it comes to risking successfully and building our courage, a key for women is to support each other, support each other, and support each other. An excellent example of this comes from one of my clients, Jackson Walker, one of the oldest, largest and most respected law firms in Texas. One might think that a law firm founded in 1887 might be less than progressive in the area of women's issues. Nothing could be farther from the truth. Not only do they actively recruit and higher top female attorneys, the firm offers significant support to a number of women's groups within the community focused on helping women reach their full potential.

Jackson Walker doesn't just talk the talk, the value they have for their female partners and their top female clients is expressed in the fact that they sponsor a weekend retreat for them at a spa. The entire weekend is crafted to create an atmosphere of women supporting, nurturing and building both personal and professional relationships. The very first evening at dinner there were conversations between clients discussing how they could potentially use each others services. New opportunities opened up for everyone attending. Men understand the value of these 'client appreciation' weekends and I'm glad to see that the male partners at Jackson Walker are supporting their partners in building "Women Supporting Women" networks.

In my programs I ask the women to brainstorm ways we can better support each other. The following are ideas that are not only discussed but proven to work:

- Encourage each other to take risks that matter.
- Start official or unofficial mentoring programs just for women. (Each person would have a mentor and be a mentor so that everyone is getting and giving.)
- Find ways to promote each other and ideas. (If all things are equal, recommend a woman.)
- Promote each other's potential specifically to others, and specifically to men.
- Ask each other about our success in meetings. (We talked earlier about how we are often advised to blow our own horn more often and how that doesn't always work very well. This idea provides for someone else to ask us about our successes in front of others, providing us the opportunity to talk about our success in a way that feels right.)
- Cut out the water cooler chatter. (Unfortunate as it is, we can all get caught in some negative conversations about others that are unnecessary. As soon as it starts, in the first 60 seconds you need to say, "Let's keep it positive." That works like a charm, everyone knows they should and they'll respect the gentle reminder. This plan doesn't work so well an hour into the conversation.
- Find a safe place to vent. (Find a partner with whom you can dump all that frustration and anger. This will provide both of you a safe place to get rid of the negative energy and leave with more productive thoughts.)

- Continue to point out each other's strengths; it will remind you of your own.
- Focus on successes.
- Accept compliments with a smile and a thank you.
- Help each other find the value in a mistake. (What's the lesson in it all? What wisdom have you gained?)
- Practice taking it less seriously. Try not to get overly emotional about everything. Work on making it fun.
- When you ask questions in meetings, give it context. (Frame the questions with, "I understand, but I'd like you to clarify..."
- Give each other the benefit of the doubt.
- Acknowledge and thank those women who support you. (If a woman recommends my program to another client and they book me, I send them a gift certificate to a spa, if possible. I feel strongly that we need to thank all those who help us.)

Equity Office Properties

Equity Office Properties (EOP) is the largest publicly held office building owner and manager in the United States. This progressive company recognizes that simply hiring talented women was not enough. The key was to create an environment in which these women would want to stay and develop their careers. Two years ago the senior management group at Equity made the strategic decision to initiate a women's initiative entitled the Women In Management Network, or WIMN. I was fortunate enough to have my program, Awaken the Leader Within —IntelligentRisking for Women, chosen to help launch their women's initiative across the country. I have now traveled to every regional Equity Office location around the country presenting my program and I have found working with this group of talented women an honor and a privilege.

Barb Kildow, Director of Investor Communications for Equity, was responsible for organizing the event for the corporate group in Chicago. Barb, having more organization in her little finger than I will possess in a lifetime, did a great job. All women were encouraged to attend. In addition to many others, Diane Morefield, Senior Vice President of Investor Relations for Equity Office and also the leader of Equity's Women in Management Network attended.

My presentations always involve a number of interactions between participants. During one interaction Barb partnered with a senior woman in the IT department. Barb's partner, the mother of four young children, was trying to build up her courage to speak with her (male) manager about the possibility of a four-day work week. She was afraid to broach the subject for fear not only that her request would be turned down but also that by even bringing up the subject, she'd be written off as "not serious" enough about her career.

She didn't realize that Barb works closely with Diane Morefield, who was herself hired years earlier on a four-day work week by Richard Kincaid, who was CFO at the time and is now president and CEO of Equity Office. Diane's flexible schedule has worked out brilliantly for her and the company. However, as in all organizations there are those who are not yet completely convinced of some of these progressive ideas. Barb urged her partner to call Diane to set up lunch and get some advice. Of course, Barb also mentioned this to Diane, who was more than happy to help in any way she could.

Diane found herself facing a challenge. It wasn't the lunch; it was the meeting she would be having on the following day. She was scheduled to give an update to all of the senior management of Equity Office on the status and successes of the Women's Initiative. It was a unique opportunity because this meeting was going to include an additional two levels of management.

It was clear from the unnamed partner's experience in IT that there were still women in the organization afraid to even broach the subject of flexible work schedules. Diane felt that if she could clearly explain the importance of the Women's Initiative during her update, that change would filter down. This meeting was Diane's chance to make a difference.

Being an accomplished, polished professional, Diane knew intuitively that she was going to have to do something different to get this group's attention. She wanted the company's senior management team to truly understand that flexible work schedules are critically important if they wanted to keep talented women at Equity Office. To make an impact, she decided to add a picture at the end of her presentation of her three children. Any woman knows that it is a risk to blur the line between professional and personal. It was a risk few men would understand, let alone ever take.

Up until the end of her presentation she wasn't sure she if she would show that last slide, knowing she could end without hitting that button one last time. As she told this story, she had me hanging onto the edge of my seat. Did she push the button? Yes. Up on the screen in front of all the executives at Equity Office was a picture of her children. She told them that only because of the flexibility of a four-day work week she was able to balance her professional and personal life, a challenge both men and women face.

I asked her why she took the risk. As Diane reflected back on the IntelligentRisking program she had attended the day before, she realized that if she wanted other women to take risks then she needed to set the example. She had to stand up for what she believed in. Diane also felt that if she could prove, on a personal level, to the management team that a flexible schedule can work, then maybe other women in the organization would be given the opportunity as well.

I asked her about the response she received. She said that several of the people in the meeting came up and congratulated her on her presentation. There is no doubt that not everyone liked her blurring that carefully guarded boundary between work and home; however, everyone walked away respecting her courage and the guts it took to take that risk.

Women supporting women is such a powerful change agent that I'd like you to commit to one action you'll take to better support other women and write it down. It may be something you'll start doing, or it may be something you'll stop doing. It may represent a huge risk or no risk. However, if each of us could commit to just one action to better help each other, then we are all ahead of the game.

Now it's time for you to commit to one action you'll take to better support other women. Please make a note of it in your journal. It may be something you'll start doing, or it may be something you'll stop doing. It may represent a huge risk or no risk. However, if each of us could commit to just one action to better help each other, then we are all ahead of the game.

One interesting postscript: Barb's partner never called Diane. Granted, she didn't know that Barb had spoken to Diane, so she may have thought Diane would be too busy to see her. I don't know why she didn't call, but if she had taken that risk it would have been a fabulous opportunity.

74. The Placebo Effect

Courage means **confidence**. In the early 1900s, doctors gave their patients pills to help them sleep, to ease depression, and to provide a pick-me-up. Often those little pills they handed out in reds and greens were simply sugar pills, or placebos. The reason they worked remarkably well was because the patients believed they were getting an actual drug and they expected it to work.

Alan Alda hosted a fascinating show on PBS on February 18, 2003. It was called "Scientific American Frontiers Program #1307 'The Wonder Pill,'" and it explored the placebo effect and its power on the human mind. Dr. Andy Leuchter conducted a study that was able to measure and quantify the placebo effect. The bottom line is that placebos have no physical effect on the body, but they do have a physiological effect that can trigger the brain, which in turn has a physiological effect that can make a disease change its course.

Dr. Leuchter's study measured the effect placebos have on brain activity through EEGs. As Alan Alda says during the show, "While it may all be in the mind, the placebo effect is real and measurable." Never does he or anyone else say that placebos work for all people. In a number of cases they had no effect; in others the positive shift was temporary. In most cases, once the patient realized it was a placebo they relapsed. However, the placebos in this study did create positive results in 40 percent of the patients. These results encourage researchers to look at a new world of possibilities in health care.

It's clear that our minds are still one of the greatest unexplored frontiers, and they hold significant power. That's why we need to focus on our accomplishments, to give ourselves credit, and to visualize ourselves as successful. Even if, at this moment, you aren't as successful as you may wish, the surest way to get there is to visualize yourself as the "successful you." That single action, the power of a vision, is the trick that enables us to open up and tap into things inside ourselves we don't yet understand.

75. How Do You Visualize Success?

Now that you've chosen your mountain, decide how you visualize success. This is a key concept. How do medical students ever make it though their internship? They visualize themselves as successfully practicing medicine and saving people's lives. So, I want your visualization to be meaningful.

In one program a lady's goal was to lose fifty pounds. Her image was getting back on the scale and the scale showing that she weighed fifty pounds less. NOT GOOD ENOUGH! That image will not keep away the chocolate donut urge in the middle of the night. So, she thought again and her new image was much more compelling. She was wearing skin tight white jeans (that's a risk for any woman). She had on strapy sandals, a midriff-baring top, and her hair was blowing in the breeze as she walked past her old boyfriend. In the background, the song "I'm too Sexy for My Shirt" was playing! Now that's a clear visualization. I told her that I thought there may be more than one mountain going on, but if it worked for her then it worked for me.

76. Do You Have the Courage?

What Is Your Courage Ratio?

Do you have the courage you need? Does your passion outweigh your fears? Even though you may feel some fear are you willing to try? If so then great, you are ready to move on. If not, then it may be time to reevaluate your mountain? Is it the right mountain? Whose mountain is it? If you still feel strongly that this is a goal you want to pursue then you will need to develop a plan to build your passion and reduce your fear.

77. What Is Your Invisible Risk?

What if You Turn Away?

If you decide you don't believe you have the courage it's going to take then before you turn back I'd like for you to ask, "What will it be like if you don't climb?" "How will you feel about yourself if you quit?" If it truly isn't your mountain and you decide to turn away then you may feel like the weight of the world has been lifted from your shoulders. If it really is your mountain and you turn away then you may have the gnawing feeling of regret and disappointment.

What if You Try and Fail?

Some people fear failing so much that they don't try which takes away confidence and adds to their fear. Ask yourself, "Even if I fail how will I feel about myself for at least trying?" "If things don't go exactly as planned will I be smarter, wiser for the experience?" "Even if it all blows up will I be proud to tell others I went for it?" What do you see as your Invisible Rewards?

78. The Ebb and Flow of Courage

Courage is an intangible that will ebb and flow as you climb. There will be days when you climb exceptionally well and you'll feel the courage of a lioness. Then there will be days that you climb very tenuously and feel as fragile as a kitten. The key is to anticipate these fluxes so that on a difficult day you don't jump to the wrong conclusion and believe that you don't have what it takes to climb this mountain.

There is a saying that "all storms pass," and they do. If you feel that you are in the middle of a dark storm, try to sit it out. Give the situation some time. Reflect on what and why things are happening and give yourself some time to think before you make a hasty decision to quit.

There is always an inherent and significant risk involved in paragliding. It would have been easy for me to say, I'm not going to fly again because it's too dangerous. However, for me there was another risk, an Invisible Risk, involved in quitting a sport I love without giving it one more chance: the risk of regret. My decision was to continue to fly, and if one day I choose to stop then I, not my fear, will be making the decision.

79. Build Your Courage Journal

Insights	Actions

Insights	Actions

Climb Strong

*"If you really want something, and really work hard,
and take advantage of opportunities,
and never give up, you will find a way."*

—*Jane Goodall*

80. Are You Willing to Let Go?

At the beginning of this book I described the crux move, the single most difficult move on any climb. It's the move you must make or you go no farther. It is very similar to the risks you need to take to reach a goal. The big difference is that on a climb the crux move is often marked along with suggestions on how to make the move. In life, that rarely happens. They tend to be surprises that are difficult to anticipate. The best advice on how to make your own crux moves is to understand that you will face them. You will be tested, perhaps to the edge of some preconceived limits, and you'll get through it.

I'm in the middle of doing research on just how much of our talents, skills, and abilities we are currently using. Initial results indicate that less than 10 percent of us are using 90 percent of our talents, skills, and abilities; 20 percent are using 80 percent; and about 60 percent of us are only using 60 percent. Clearly we have more potential to make those crux moves than we may realize.

The Monster Within is often made up of a combination of fear, anger, and ego. It is one of the most dangerous and insidious of the Invisible Risks. Even when you start out with self-assurance, it can sneak up on you. Obstacles that shake your confidence allow self-doubt to creep into your thinking and rumble around in your psyche, jeopardizing your mission. The Cowardly Lion, the Tin Man, and the Scarecrow each suffered because they doubted themselves. They went searching elsewhere for what they had inside themselves all along. Even though you may not be able to anticipate what your crux move might be, if you understand that you will face one then you won't be quite so quick to listen to the whispers of the monster.

The National Anthem

Janece, who worked in the state government, was attending one of my programs. Her mountain was to start a wedding planning business, but she felt she didn't have the courage to start. When I asked her why that particular business, she said she just loved everything about weddings and, in fact, she often sang at weddings. Some of Janece's coworkers were nearby, and they all started talking about how beautifully she sang. Out of the blue, I asked her if she'd sing something for us.

Janece came up to the front of the room, got on stage, took the microphone, and with no advanced warning, no preparation, and no accompaniment began to sing "The Star Spangled Banner." It was the most beautiful and the most moving rendition of our national anthem that I have heard. Nearly everyone in the room (all women) had tears in their eyes when she finished. It was truly an amazing experience.

Talk about risk being subjective. There is no way in the world I would have been willing to stand up in front of a group and sing anything. I do not have the courage, talent, or passion. My guess is that out of a couple hundred people no one else in that room would have been willing to take the risk of singing, either. Yet, many of us in that room would and have taken the risk of starting our own business, the risk that Janece was afraid to take. Risk taking is a fascinating subject.

The most amazing thing of all was that at the end of the program, three women came up to Janece and asked her to call them because they wanted to help her start her business and each was planning a wedding.

By declaring your mountain and taking a risk, doors open. Interestingly it's hard to tell who it is that's going to help you as you climb your mountain. Sometimes it's family, sometimes it's friends, and sometimes all those people you thought you could count on fade away. Just then, along comes a stranger, an angel, someone to help you. The key is, no one can help you climb if you're not out there on your mountain trying.

Not believing in yourself may be the greatest risk you'll ever take.

What to Do When You Don't Know What to Do

What should a person do when she doesn't know what to do? If you truly don't know what move to make, try to give yourself some time to think it through. If you don't have that luxury then the best course of action is to trust your gut. There is no one else out there who knows the situation better than you, so act on your intuition. You will most likely do the right thing for the right reason and in the smartest way. Then you can always trust that you've done the best you could at the time with what you knew.

81. Are You Willing to Embrace Your Adventure?

Katherine

Who knows what adventures your mountain will bring? There's no point in climbing anything if you aren't having fun. Since life doesn't seem to go out of its way to make anything easy for us, it's up to us to seize the day. As a wish grantor for the Make-A-Wish Foundation, I consider all my wish children to be special; however, as we talk about embracing your adventure I'm reminded of Katherine.

I love to make things special for the kids, and I often partner on granting wishes with Brian O'Malley. The day we went to deliver Katherine's wish trip to Disney World I had picked up a tiara and a magic wand for her. Sometimes Make-A-Wish sends some little gifts along like stationary, stickers, or books. We were very surprised when she opened up a compete set of little girls' makeup all in a shade of bright blue. Well we all know that girls, no matter their age, like to try on new makeup immediately.

Katherine had a disease that was deteriorating her spine along which created additional complications, so she used a wheel chair and had limited dexterity with her hands. She already had on her tiara and was holding her wand, so she looked like quite a princess. That's when she asked me to help out with the "makeover." I'm certainly not an experienced cosmetologist so we quickly had blue sparkle powder and eye shadow all over both of us. Then I started on her nails with blue nail polish. Once I finished she looked down at her manicure. She frowned, and not being able to remember my name she said, "Princess Servant, you missed a spot." I fixed it, and she wheeled herself up to the full-length mirror in the hallway to survey the results of her makeover. That's when she said, "Look out Cinderella, there's a new princess coming to town!" It was a magical moment.

82. Fall Forward

"Nothing in life is to be feared, it is only to be understood."
—Marie Curie

Will you make mistakes? Probably. The key is to learn how to make mistakes that take you closer not farther from your goal. I'm convinced that one reason why I've found the success that I have is that I am very good at making mistakes. Well, practice makes perfect and I've certainly had my share of practice. Over time, with a lot of mistakes to learn from you begin to figure out which mistakes to make. Don't be afraid to make mistakes; just learn to make really smart ones so you can figure out the best path. Many times it's easier and quicker to try something, learn, and recover than it is to try to analyze the correct thing to do. I look at life like this: I'm 5 feet 6 inches tall, and if I make a mistake and fall forward, then I'm almost 6 feet closer to my goal.

It helps if we can look at mistakes as merely outcomes that don't currently fit your expectations. Or consider the old axiom, Solutions only redefine the problem.

83. The Butterfly Effect

In 1960, Edward Lorenz was a meteorologist at M.I.T. responsible for predicting weather patterns. Computers had recently been introduced and in an effort to expedite the process he decided to round off a number in one of his calculations by one-thousandth. He assumed that there would be no significant variation in his predictions. That small change was the equivalent of the puff of wind created by one butterfly's wing. That insignificant change significantly altered the projection creating a tropical storm. Since then the concept of a single action generating the momentum to create a significant change has been called the Butterfly Effect.

If you have ever mentioned an interest just once to family and friends — let's say you like miniature clowns as my Mother once did — then you have seen the power of this effect. For years and years thereafter Mom received miniature clowns from everyone. She got them on calendars, mugs, cards, and posters, as well as an assortment of small clowns and larger ones to fill shelf after shelf. You will not believe how many ugly clown products are available, and now my Mother has them all over her house. I've come to the conclusion that the attack of the clowns will never end. Even when she began telling people that she no longer liked clowns nor had room for any more, they still continue to show up. Her love of clowns is slowly transforming itself into an intense dislike for them. She swears they multiply in the dark as she continues to find them and put them into her garage sales.

How big of a first step you take toward climbing your mountain is not as important as taking that first step. The momentum you create by declaring your mountain to others (for example, that you like miniature clowns), by checking out that one book, or by making that first call is significant. That one action does indeed create a ripple effect that will help pull/push you toward your goal.

If we look at this concept in the bigger picture, consider that the one risk you take today, the one mountain you climb, will create new and significant opportunities for you in the future.

84. One Step at a Time

The key to starting is that first step. Think of one action that you are willing to take within the next week. Decide who would make the best climbing partner for you and commit to them that one action you are going to take in the next seven days. This partnership will help put some positive pressure on you to make it happen. While doing a program for Equity Office Properties I asked a woman what one step she would take. Her answer was profound. She said, "It isn't a question of what I will do. It's a matter of what I'll stop doing."

It doesn't matter what your one action is and it doesn't matter how big of step it is. What matters is that you take action to start building your momentum.

85. Will You Climb Strong?

In rock climbing, when you tie the rope from you to your partner you're saying, "I trust you with my life." There is a certain seriousness about that, and there is an unwritten procedure. Once each person ties their end of the rope into their own harness they double-check their own and each other's knots for safety. Whoever is going to climb first is the climber and whoever is holding the rope to keep them safe is the person belaying. When the climber is ready she says, "Belay on." When the belayer is ready, she responds with, "On belay." Then when the climber is actually going to start climbing she says, "Climbing." Then the belayer is to say, "Climb on." This is the code. It's not a lot of words, and one would think they are fairly easy to remember, unless you're scared out of your mind like I was the first time I went climbing.

I don't know what you do but sometimes when I'm really nervous and I can't remember what I'm suppose to say, I just make things up. That's what happened that first day. I was belaying, and even though I wasn't the one climbing, it would be my turn to climb next, and that was scary. My partner was ready and said "On belay." I responded appropriately with "Belay on." So far, so good. But when my partner said "Climbing!" I realized that I was going to be responsible for this person's life I totally locked up. It created an embarrassing silence. When he turned to look at me I just blurted out "Climb Strong!" It came out more like a question, but I thought it was pretty close to what I was suppose to say and it sort of rhymed. I remember my partner giving me a very odd look. I knew that he knew I was really scared. All he said was, "That's a new one." I'm sure he saw what little confidence I had left crumble, so he quickly added, "I like it, it's different, but please say it like you mean it."

I took that as a serious vote of confidence, so I said in my bravest voice, "Climb strong!" I still use that when I climb, and what is cool is that I now hear others saying it too. I like it because it sums it all up, the excitement, the fear, the determination, the confidence, the trust, and the thrill of going for it. "Climb Strong!" is how I end every program, and it's on all my marketing materials. I've taught my boys to use it when they climb. It's special to me and will always remind me to act with courage and conviction.

86. What Are You Waiting For?

It's Time to Climb!

You have chosen your mountain, planned your route and built your courage. The only thing left is to make your move and Climb Strong!

87. Climb Strong Journal

Insights	*Actions*

Insights	Actions

The Critical Questions

*"I had reasoned this out in my mind, there was one of two things
I had a right to, liberty or death; if I could not have one,
I would have the other."*
—*Harriett Tubman*

88. Twelve Critical IntelligentRisking Questions

IntelligentRisking Is an Art

The beauty of IntelligentRisking is that it offers a new perspective as it simplifies the often complicated and convoluted process of risk taking. In this book we have explored the four IntelligentRisking strategies and a number of questions you may want to ask yourself. There is no right or wrong answer. There is no foolproof system to know for sure if you are taking the right risk. However, the thought process you have just gone through regarding your mountain, your route, your courage, and how you'll climb has dramatically increased your odds for success. The reality of IntelligentRisking is that if you choose the right risk and you take it in the smartest way possible, even if that risk doesn't turn out as planned it usually still turns out.

"A life spent in making mistakes is not only more honorable but more useful than a life spent in doing nothing."
—George Bernard Shaw

In an effort to further simplify the process I've narrowed down all that we've discussed into the twelve critical questions that every woman should ask before she risks:

Choose Your Mountain

1. What's my mountain?

2. Whose mountain is it?

3. How do I define success?

Plan Your Route

4. What's my route?

5. What's my backup plan?

Build Your Courage

6. Have I faced my fears?

7. How do I visualize success?

8. Do I have the courage?

9. What's my Invisible Risk?

Climb Strong!

10. Am I willing to let go?

11. Will I climb strong?

12. What am I waiting for?

89. Critical Questions Journal

Insights	Actions

Insights	*Actions*

The Next Horizon

What do you see when you get to the top of a mountain?
More mountains.

90. Rest, Renew and Reflect

Once you've finished your climb it's time to rest, renew, and reflect. At the end of any climb, no matter the outcome, you have changed, and it's time to ask yourself: What did you learn? What wisdom did you gain? What would you do again? What would you change? What memories will you cherish? What stories will make you laugh? It's also time to recalibrate by understanding how you've changed and to incorporate those changes into your life in a positive way.

Once you have had time to adapt and adopt to your experience it will be time to think about the next horizon. What's out there for you? What has your passion now? All of us at different points in our lives struggle with the question, "What's next?" Olympic athletes and astronauts often face depression because they aren't sure what a person should do once they've walked on the moon or won a gold medal.

The key to risk taking is that the more risks you take, the more you learn. The more you learn the better you become at taking risks. The better you get, the more confidence you gain. The more confidence you gain, the more courage you have. The more courage you have, the better you get at taking risks.

This book isn't about taking risks just for the sake of taking risks. It's about awakening the leader within so that you see your potential as well as your ability to climb those mountains that will make a difference in your life.

91. Why Are You Still Reading This Book?

You have what it takes, so make your move and climb stong!

92. Next Horizon Journal

Insights	Actions

Insights	*Actions*

Best Practices

"Somewhere out in this audience may even be someone who will one day follow my footsteps, and preside over the White House as the president's spouse. I wish him well!"

—Barbara Bush

This section is an additional supplement to the book. It supports yet is not a critical part of the IntelligentRisking for Women process. This section explores men and women's leadership styles as well as the what, why, and how we look at risk differently.

93. Powerful Leadership Styles

This section will look at "best practices," successful leadership traits for both men and women, with the intent of learning which, if any, we may want to incorporate into our own leadership style. We will also look at some of the basic differences between how men and women look at risk, why these differences exist, and how to deal with them.

There is enormous value in understanding and developing your own individual leadership style, one that feels natural and complements your own personality. This is true whether you have a thousand people reporting to you or if the only person reporting to you is you.

I met Cynthia Comparin, C.E.O. and President of her own company, Animato, at the networking weekend the Jackson Walker law firm sponsored this year in San Antonio. Animato, is a 100 million dollar business that focuses on people and technology in motion specializing in financial and human resource management software?

When you meet Cynthia you can see immediately that she is a dynamo focused on the big picture. Over dinner even her friends teased her about how she doesn't like to be bothered with the details to the point that Sheila, her personal assistant virtually runs her life for her. I asked Cynthia how she came to start a business that is all about details when she so obviously disliked doing detail work so much. Her answer was that as a former Group CFO for EDS she learned how to do detail better than anyone.

Cynthia explained that even though that detail mindset is not her natural style she saw it as the price of admission to play the game. It was the foundation she needed to launch her own new game. She still likes, wants, needs and expects detail from those who work for her but now she can move beyond doing details herself to focus on her strength of strategic business development.

The irony is that before you can move into your own natural style you must earn the right by being good at what you do and to get good at what you do you must understand what leadership skills are required to build your own foundation. Some of those may come naturally and some may not. This is when you must decide to accept, reject or change to include those other traits. As with most everything in life developing your own leadership style is a dynamic process that evolves over time.

When deciding if you want to adapt the leadership traits required for success within your organization one question to ask is if they are positive, healthy traits. Most of the time they will be; however, it's important to stay true to yourself. That is exactly how Cynthia Cooper of Worldcom, Coleen Rowley of the FBI and Sherron Watkins of Enron landed on the cover of Time magazine as persons of the year in 2002. They were not willing to accept or adapt to what their organizations demanded and instead held true to themselves and became whistleblowers.

I recently had a conversation about this very subject with a friend of mine, Debra Baldwin, a senior vice president at the University of Phoenix, the largest private university in the world. She has a wealth of professional experience and has been a key player in helping the University of Phoenix achieve its phenomenal growth. In 2002 she was selected as a Woman of Distinction by the Mile High Council of Girl Scouts. This year she was chosen Business Woman of the Year by the *Denver Business Journal.*

When Debra and I began discussing this subject I asked her what advice she gives other women regarding leadership and risk. Her response was immediate: "Live a balanced life that allows you to celebrate your full potential in every aspect of what is vital to you; that will require some degree of risk. Success often means the risk of criticism. It is hard to be invisible and lead at the same time. Exposure to criticism is the cost of admission to top levels of the organization so risk intelligently. Never compromise ethics, integrity, values, matters of compliance, or the hearts and minds of others. Most importantly never ever settle for a mediocre life."

94. Gender Difference Theories

The most successful managers in the future will be those who are willing to go beyond their own comfort zones and take the risk of expanding their professional competencies to include skills from both male and female perspectives. They are the ones who will bring value to their organizations and develop the intellectual capital and management talent that they can capitalize on in any environment. Since there are not too many men's groups requesting programs on this topic, we'll focus on how we as women can become more successful leaders.

Many theories have been offered as to why there are gender differences in leadership. The two most prevalent are the psychological and situational theories. The psychological theory emphasizes the different outlook, attitudes, and values implanted in men and women during their development and socialization. Women tend to demonstrate greater affiliation, attachment, cooperation, and nurturance, while men tend to demonstrate more independent, instrumentally oriented, and competitive behaviors.

The situational theory argues that gender differences are few and largely an artifact of differences in opportunity, power, and lack of representation in business and organizational settings. I'm convinced that the reality lies in a combination of the two.

Still other theories propose that there are no differences between men and women and that it all comes down to the differences between individuals. However, being a single mother of three teenage boys, I'm here to tell you that based on firsthand experience, there are many, many distinctive differences between males and females. Testosterone literally drips off the walls at my house. A typical conversation with my boys goes something like this:

Mom: "Why did you push him?"
Son: "He was standing there."

Mom: "Can't we just enjoy the game?"
Son: "It's not fun if you don't win."

Mom: "We need to talk about this."
Son: "There's nothing to talk about."

There has been a tremendous amount of research done by some very qualified individuals on the differences between men and women and why more capable women are not achieving the levels of success in businesses. I've done a significant amount of quantitative and qualitative research, in addition to reading dozens of books and hundreds of articles on the subject. Yet, whenever I hear someone touting research statistics I'm reminded of the old adage, "Figures don't lie, liars figure." I don't mean to imply that everyone is intentionally skewing the results to support their own theory. We just seem to have a way of making information fit our needs. Even when results are reported accurately, you still can't always trust what people say they will do in a given situation.

Take, for example, a situation I encountered at Mattel Toys. I was involved in new product development, and since "traditional" toys were appealing to a younger and younger audience, we were losing a significant amount of market share.

We were trying to develop products that would appeal to older children. A no-brainer was to develop a funky boom box. Market research at the time was huge at Mattel, so we brought in a number of teens and asked them their opinions of what features they felt kids would want in a product.

One specific question we asked was, "What color would sell the most?" Their overwhelming response was neon "hot" green. At the end of the session, as they were leaving, we invited them to take a boom box as a thank you gift for their time. Every one of them took a black one. From that day on I've always said, "There is research and then there is research. There is what we say we'll do in any given situation, and then there is what we actually do." Each of us needs to come up with our own conclusions regarding the information others propose based on what rings true to us.

Based on what I have experienced myself, what others have experienced, and what I've studied, I don't believe that there is any one theory that explains gender differences. I think that there are a multitude of factors that combine in unique ways that contribute to our struggle to find meaningful success. They come into play in different combinations according to each of our unique situations at the time. They also vary in degree based on our specific industry, company, team, environment, background, experience, and personality. Some of these factors are within our control, and some are not.

For the purposes of this book, I've chosen to concentrate on two reasons behind some of the more significant gender differences: (1) the continued gulf in the understanding of the differences between men and women in business, and (2) the need for women to take Intelligent Risks. I've chosen these two because they are both extremely important, highly pervasive, and within our control.

Women represent an incredible amount of intellectual capital. Corporations and other companies are beginning to understand that they have made a tremendous investment in us and can no longer afford to lose us to other companies or careers by not meeting our needs. They understand that it is through accumulating and holding on to this intellectual capital that they'll be able to establish and maintain their competitive edge. They're now becoming focused on finding a way to make it work. For the forward-thinking organizations such as Deloitte & Touche and Equity Office Properties, it has become a business imperative because they are now correlating diversity success into increased profits to the bottom line.

Because organizations are beginning to understand what a valuable resource we are, it's now up to us to clearly understand what we want and need to achieve the kinds of meaningful success we're after. Although we'll touch on this in generalities, the interactive pieces should help you relate to all of the information as we discuss you, your life, and your goals.

95. Successful Leadership Traits

Men

Men do a lot of things right, so let's take a look at what leadership traits we most admire and respect from our male counterparts. As we look at some of the differences between men and women we will be making some very broad generalizations. Some of what we discuss will be true about some men all the time, all men some of the time, and no man all of the time. There is no intent to show any lack of respect or admiration for our male counterparts. I hope you (as well as the many males reading this) will accept these generalizations of both men and women in the spirit in which it is intended.

Given all the disclaimers, groups usually come up with a pretty similar list of qualities that we admire about men as listed below. You may want to add some of your own thoughts about some of the qualities and characteristics that you admire.

1. Don't take things too personally. Can disagree in a meeting and still be friends.
2. Big-picture oriented
3. Competitive/assertive
4. Risk takers
5. Individualistic
6. Work hard/play hard
7. Good old boys club
8. Self-promotion/talk about accomplishments
9. Objective/not overly emotional
10. Focus on successes
11. Direct/they ask for what they want and expect to get it
12. Focused

Women

Women share many of the traits we've listed for men; however, there are some traits that are unique to us. Let's look at what we admire and respect the most about ourselves. If we've missed anything please include it on your own list.

1. Sensitive
2. Intuitive
3. Empathetic
4. Flexible
5. Team player/collaborative
6. Work hard
7. Nurturing
8. Modest
9. Passionate
10. Effective communicators
11. Listener/tactful
12. Multi-tasking

Let me mention here that women have come a long way. A study done by the *Harvard Business Review* in 1965 entitled "Are Women Executives People?" showed that 32 percent of all male managers believed that women's fundamental biological makeup made them unfit for management. My first professional job was with Hallmark Cards, and I was in the Chicago branch office. I was at that time the only woman in any type of management position. All the other women in the office were secretaries. It was 1974, and if there was a meeting, I automatically got everyone coffee. I did this of my own free will. No one asked me to; in fact, it would never have crossed the men's minds to ask me, it was just expected. I wasn't resentful because I didn't know any better. Two years later I felt differently. I made the decision to no longer get everyone's coffee. I felt that by taking a stand, I was taking a risk. Today, this would never be an issue.

My friend Valari recalls that she was delighted when she was first offered a position with Mattel Toys back in 1968. It was a sales position and considered a plumb job with a great company. It was during a time when most women with careers were secretaries, nurses, teachers, stewardesses, or whatever else was considered the norm for women who wanted or needed to work.

Valari was given the title of "retail specialist," a sales territory, and a sales goal. After a short training period and a few sales meetings later, she realized that all the other women working in sales were "retail specialists" while the men with the same job were called "retail merchandisers." The difference was that although the job, the territories, the sales goals, and the expectations were the same, the retail specialists were "nonexempt" while the retail merchandisers were "exempt." This meant that although they were doing the same job, the men were given company cars, higher wages, and more benefits.

Needless to say, this struck Valari and most of the other women as unjust and discriminatory. However, because most of the women were grateful to have this job, no one wanted to create a wave and rock the boat. That was until a sales meeting when the senior vice president of sales and marketing asked Valari how she enjoyed her job. Before answering, she realized she had a choice. She could say the politically right thing, or take a risk and tell the truth, that she felt it was unfair that women were doing the same job as the men, for substantially lower pay and benefits.

She took the risk and outlined exactly how she felt, while at the same time wondering where she'd be working next. She didn't lose her job. In fact, at the next sales meeting, the same senior vice president made the announcement that all sixty of the retail specialists were being promoted to retail merchandisers.

In the decades since then, there's been a great increase in the number of women getting degrees in science and mathematics. In some colleges the women outnumber the men. Things have gotten better, and they will no doubt continue to improve.

Unfortunately, it's still tough in the corporate world for women. It's hard to get equal opportunities and equal pay, particularly at the higher levels. Like it or not, the game is still dominated and run by men with a man's mindset, predispositions, and prejudices. That is why to this day very often men are judged on their potential and women judged on their performance. It's helpful to understand why and how to operate in this environment.

96. The Differences

As we look at the preceding lists, we see some opposing qualities that are on both lists as traits we respect. For example, we admire men's ability to self-promote, yet we respect our ability to be modest. We like the assertive nature of men, but we're proud of our ability to nurture.

The differences in what we admire can be extremely confusing. Some of us have been coached along the way to "blow our own horn" more often. Sometimes it works and sometimes it blows back up in our face. Why? Significant research has been done that makes a substantial case for how being more assertive works for women. Then again, it has been equally substantiated by research that being assertive doesn't work for women. With so much conflicting data, what are we to do? The key is to be assertive in a way that feels natural and plays into your own individual style. Don't force it. If it doesn't work for you, then it won't feel right to anyone else.

It may help to take a look at some of the reasons we're so different from men. Some of you may be very familiar with this information and you may want to use it just as a reminder. For some of you this information will be brand new and provide a new frame of reference from which to better understand what and why things happen the way they do.

Earlier this year I took my oldest son, Connor, on a business trip with me to Boston, and one evening we went to see Rob Becker's "Defending the Caveman" show. His program is an extremely funny take on the differences between men and women.

In the show he asks you to imagine six men sitting around a bowl of chips. One of them says to the others, "Hey, we're out of chips." How many men jump up to fill the bowl? Of course, you already know: none. We have now stepped into the world of male negotiation, which goes something like this: Male #1 says, "I'm not going to get the chips, I filled the bowl the first time." Male #2 responds, "Well, I'm not going to get them; I brought the bowl." Male #3 counters with, "I'm not going to get them; I brought the beer." Says Male #4, "I'm not going to get them; it's my house." On it goes until one of three things happens: they all starve to death, one poor soul finally gives in, or the host's wife comes in and makes him do it. Either way, the man who has to get more chips is the loser. Even so, there are no hard feelings, no grudges, between the men.

Now imagine six women sitting around the chip bowl. Someone mentions they're out of chips. How many women get up to fill the bowl? Of course, all six. And if one didn't? What if one woman sat there and waited while all the others got up? She'd be the loser, though a loser of a different kind. We all know the rules for this type of social interaction; in the end whether it's a group of men or a group of women the chip bowl usually gets refilled, but it's a perfect example of the differences between men and women..

As my son and I watched the rest of the show we both laughed until we had tears running down our faces. (Editorial correction requested by my son: I had tears running down my face and he just had something in his eye.)

97. Team/Individual

Today's organizations talk about TEAMS, but most still reward individuals. Women tend to talk in terms of "we" while men talk in terms of "I." We make a tactical decision, for the good of the project, we share information and resources, then instead of being looked upon as a **strategic team player**, we're called "**nice**." Women are good at relationship skills, but this is often misunderstood and viewed as "women being friendly." If a woman makes a decision based on her instincts, she does not get the same respect as a man making a decision based on his gut.

Young boys get together and immediately start bragging about who's the best, who should be the leader. They start reliving their exploits and retelling their successes. They tell each other that they're the smartest, the strongest, etc. Finally someone is chosen to be the leader. They start the game King of the Hill, and the rest of the boys try to push the leader off of the hill so that they can be king.

Imagine a group of young girls getting together and one of them saying, "I think I should be the leader because I'm the smartest, the strongest, etc." She'd be seen as pushy and arrogant. How long would she even be allowed in the group?

Through games like King of the Hill, boys learn to promote their strengths and at all costs hide their weaknesses. A show of weakness means an attack from the group. Women, in contrast, learn how to be inclusive by playing down their strengths and being open about their weaknesses. (For more on this, read *The Power of Talk: Who Gets Heard and Why,* by Deborah Tannen.)

My boys were fighting the other day. When I came into the room to find out what was going on, one of them said, "He started it when he hit me back." I realized that this is the universal way boys and men look at the world and I personally believe it accounts for how they get into so many wars.

98. Self-Promotion/Modesty

"I would venture to guess that Anon, who wrote
so many poems without signing them, was a woman."

—*Virginia Woolfe*

When I first started speaking about IntelligentRisking, I said very little about my professional experiences with Coors, Disney, Hallmark, and Mattel. I was afraid that I'd appear too egocentric if I talked about myself. My clients were confused and disappointed. They had to point out to me that the reason they hired me was so that I would share some of my successes. It's amazing how ingrained humility is in women. Even though it's something we admire, it can certainly get in our way.

Psychologist Laurie Heatherington and her colleagues reported the results of their interesting research in the journal Sex Roles (Vol. 29, 1993). They asked hundreds of incoming college students to predict what grades they would get in their first year. Some subjects were asked to make their predictions privately by writing them down and placing them in an envelope; others were asked to make their predictions publicly, in the presence of a researcher. The results showed that more women than men predicted lower grades for themselves if they made their predictions publicly. If they made their predictions privately, the predictions were the same as those of the men — and the same as their actual grades. What could have been interpreted as a lack of confidence was actually the act of being modest.

99. Minimizing Doubts/ Minimizing Certainty

My brother, Doug, has always said, "Better to be thought a fool than to open your mouth and prove it." This provides a powerful insight into why men don't ask for directions. If they ask, they prove they don't know something and they reveal a weakness.

It's important for women to understand how men view others who ask questions. If you are in a meeting and ask lots of questions, men generally will assume you don't know as much as the others who aren't asking questions. This may or may not be true. It may be that the others are just too afraid to ask. I have also found that women tend to ask questions for clarification and not because they don't know. Women will also ask questions to help out others if they feel not everyone understands.

Women are quick to say, "I'm sorry" while a man is quick to say, "I'll accept your apology." It's very difficult for a man to admit fault if he doesn't have to. This all comes back to men's conditioning to play up their strengths and hide any and all of their weaknesses. A man equates revealing a weakness as leaving himself vulnerable to an attack.

100. Competitive Ritual/ Complimentary Ritual

Many men have their rituals of combat. They love to spar in a meeting. They like to throw out an idea (it might even be one they don't really even believe in), heatedly argue it, and then go out together for a beer. Most women just don't get this. We want to be able to do that and not take any of it personally, but it just isn't what we're used to.

We do, however, have our rituals of compliments. Let's imagine that Linda walks up to JoAnn and says, "Your hair looks great today." Now JoAnn responds to Linda and says, "I love that new jacket, you look great in it." All women know how this ritual works. Men seldom understand this ritual.

In the business world this ritual of compliments works a little differently because it collides with a man's tendency to look for a one-up position. A friend of mine was part of a team who flew to New York to give a major client presentation. She thought everyone had done a good job with their presentation but felt that hers was the best. Her boss had even told her that she had done the best job.

tion. She thought everyone had done a good job with their presentation but felt that hers was the best. Her boss had even told her that she had done the best job.

On the return flight to Los Angeles, she sat next to a male associate. Once they were settled on the plane she turned to her associate and said something like, "I thought you did a really good job on your presentation." He said, "Thank you." Then she waited. Now, we all know what he was suppose to say, right? He said nothing. That was when my friend made a huge tactical error by asking, "What did you think of my presentation." He then launched into a two-hour evaluation of her presentation and what she should have done differently. He took the one-up position that she had handed him. Next time she'll be much clearer about what she wants by asking, "What did you like about my presentation?"

This story is a good example of how men are conditioned to quickly accept compliments, whether they deserve them or not. I'm convinced this is a huge asset. Women, in comparison, have been conditioned to play down, deny, or even reject compliments, even when they are well deserved. It goes back to our early years, when we wanted to fit in and find ways to be inclusive. By the time we're adults we all know better. As I talk to senior professional women all over the country, they assure me that they are way beyond this challenge. They all tell me that they are just as quick as a man to accept a compliment. Well, maybe they are, and maybe they aren't.

I was having breakfast with my friend Leslie Carlson, who at the time was the Vice President of Operations for Destination Hotels & Resorts in Denver. We were talking about this very subject when another friend of mine approached our table with her husband to say hello. As I was introducing Leslie, I mentioned that she was a marketing genius. Her immediate response was to say, "No, I'm not." The immediate reaction of my friend's husband was to say, "I have never received a compliment like that in my life; you should accept it." I'm convinced that these social patterns run more deeply than we believe.

101. Focus on Success/ Focus on Failure

Check a man's to-do list and it may have ten things on it. Check a woman's to-do list and it may have a hundred and ten things on it. At the end of the day if a man gets seven things done, he is proud of himself. He may take the evening off and celebrate in some way. At the end of the day if we look at our list and we've accomplished ninety-five things, how often do we take the evening off to bask in our success? Never. We don't take a single minute to tell anyone about all that we've accomplished. Instead we work until we drop into bed exhausted but dwelling on those five things we didn't get done. THIS IS NOT HEALTHY. The ability to focus on success is imbedded into men from an early age. This is a skill women need to acquire.

Not only do we focus on what we didn't get done, women have a tendency to devalue our own accomplishments. So, in addition to focusing on what we didn't get done, we tend to then think, gosh I really didn't get anything important done today. The reality is that we still got ninety-five things done and yet not only aren't we giving ourselves credit for them, somehow we lose credit because those things weren't really important.

My research tells me that one of the key reasons we do this is because we aren't really clear on how we define success. One minute we define success in a more holistic and qualitative way, which may include a very strong nurturing role in which we are trying to create a family meal, make cookies, run errands, shuttle service, clean, etc. Then the next minute we may define success in a more quantifiable way, where we need to make a very clear, calculable difference in which we measure success by income, power, and status.

Either definition of success or a combination works very well. What doesn't work as well is when we aren't sure of how we define success or we rely on someone else's definition of success for us. What happens then is that we swing back and forth between definitions. If this happens, then we find ourselves getting ninety-five things done during the day that are important to us and yet at the end of the day when we start looking for quantifiable, measurable successes, we come up short. It is critical that we are clear on how we define success.

One week after she attended my IntelligentRisking program, a woman e-mailed me saying that it had taken her ten years to get the vice presidency that she wanted and one week to figure out that wasn't what she really wanted at all. The fact that women own 66% of all home-based business reinforces that we struggle to find success in a traditional environment and have decided to find success on our own terms.

This tendency of ours to downplay our successes is the reason I want you to list every one of your strengths and only a few of your weaknesses. If I don't ask women to look at their leadership style in this way, they often end up focusing on the negatives. Yet, to be successful at anything it helps to visualize yourself as successful.

102. Setting Yourself Up for Success/ Setting Yourself Up Not to Fail

We discussed the situational theories earlier, and they certainly come into play. It is naturally easier for men to understand men than it is for men to understand women. This holds true in reverse. Given that the majority of senior positions are held by men, it is easier for them to imagine how a man with a wife and three children can get the job done than it is for them to imagine how a woman with a husband and three children can get the job done. Let's face it: Most women still bear the burden of keeping up the home and raising the children. So, with all the qualifications being equal, the edge will usually go to the man.

Many men will hesitate to give a woman a plumb assignment, believing that women just end up leaving the company to have children. The woman, fully qualified for these assignments, sees herself passed up time and time again, gets frustrated, and leaves the company. Her manager then says, "I told you so."

At the same time, women often set up their own scenarios for failure. Time and time again I hear women saying that they were offered a promotion and weren't sure they were ready for it. Because they didn't want to set themselves up for failure, they passed on the opportunity, only to watch a man with less knowledge, talent, and experience come in and take the job.

103. IntelligentRisking and Women

One key to IntelligentRisking is self-confidence, because no one can predict the course or outcome of a risk. That means that to risk, you must have a significant amount of confidence and be willing to trust your own ability and resourcefulness to see the risk through — no matter what.

I'm often asked if men have a better knack for taking risks. My answer is "No, they do not." However, they are often more willing to take risks because of their high self-confidence level. They have spent their lives focusing on their strengths and enhancing them. They have spent a lifetime minimizing their weaknesses. They have been conditioned to be competitive and fight for their ideas. They constantly visualize themselves as King of the Hill.

The reality is that people (men or women) who continually see themselves in this type of successful light tend to have more confidence, real or imagined so they are more willing to give it a go. The goal of this book is to help women risk up to their ability.

Women want to contribute in an effective and meaningful way without losing ourselves. We know we're bright enough. We know we have the education. We know we have the tools we need. The irony is that women have what they need to risk, and yet it is difficult to hold on to the self-confidence we require if we continually underplay our successes, devalue our accomplishments, and sell ourselves short. These tendencies create a phenomenon where women who have the talent, the skill and the courage to risk hold back because they can't see their own potential.

The reality is that we already have what it takes to be successful risk takers. All we need is to be clear about what we want, focus on our strengths, and take intelligent risks to get there. IntelligentRisking is intended to help you set yourself up for success. This book was written to help you start taking those risks that will make a positive difference... To Awaken the Leader Within.

"Sometimes I feel discriminated against,
but it does not make me angry.

It merely astonishes me.
How can they deny themselves the pleasure of my company?

It's beyond me."

— *Zora Neale Hurston*

104. Best Practices Journal

Insights	Actions

Insights	Actions